AF255205

Animal Afterlife?

Animal Afterlife?

A History of Hope

Betsy Clark George

WIPF & STOCK · Eugene, Oregon

Wipf and Stock Publishers
199 W. 8th Ave., Suite 3
Eugene, OR 97401

www.wipfandstock.com

PAPERBACK ISBN: 978-1-6667-4009-7
HARDCOVER ISBN: 978-1-6667-4010-3
EBOOK ISBN: 978-1-6667-4011-0

Cataloguing-in-Publication data:

Names: George, Betsy Clark [author].

Title: Animal afterlife? : a history of hope / by Betsy Clark George.

Description: Eugene, OR: Wipf and Stock 2023 | Includes bibliographical references and index.

Identifiers: ISBN 978-1-6667-4009-7 (paperback) | ISBN 978-1-6667-4010-3 (hardcover) | ISBN 978-1-6667-4011-0 (ebook)

Subjects: LCSH: Animals—Religious aspects—Christianity | Animals (Philosophy)—History | Heaven—Christianity | Eschatology | Animal welfare—Religious aspects—Christianity | Human-animal relationships—Christianity

Classification: BT746 G46 2023 (print) | BT746 (ebook)

03/28/23

Dedicated to mite and mammoth, and all
creatures in between. Zillions of them.
I love them. Only their Creator knows them
individually, and He loves them with everlasting
love. Thus throughout eternity they will sing,
*To Him be praise and honor and glory
and power for ever and ever.*
Revelation 5:13

Contents

Preface

> How many are your works, O LORD!
> In wisdom you made them all;
> the earth is full of your creatures.
> There is the sea, vast and spacious,
> teeming with creatures beyond number—
> living things both large and small.
>
> —PSALM 104:24–25

SINCE THE BEGINNING OF time, animals have played an important role in human life. They have been laborers, sacrifices, companions, nuisances, as well as objects of science, sport, art, and nutrition. Without them, life would be quite empty, or at least much less interesting. But what about life in the hereafter? Is it for humans only? Are animals excluded or included? Do animals have souls? *Immortal* souls?

The topic of immortality has generated these questions off and on for centuries and the discussions are fascinating. Reflecting on the intriguing ideas delineated by sages of the past, it is a sad commentary on contemporary culture that many earlier theologians and philosophers have been forgotten. This book focuses on a variety of such authors throughout western history, and examines some of their most intricate and authoritative possibilities. Early Hebrew concepts, Greek philosophy, New Testament statements, Roman Catholic theology, and Protestant opinions impacted by scientific theories all offer thoughtful responses to the questions raised above.

Although today's society may be less familiar with the concept of immortality than in the past, it is truly encouraging to realize that current interest in the well-being of non-human creatures is more lively, pertinent, imaginative, and practical than in any previous era. May this love for our fellow-travelers through life continue to increase with both knowledge and joy!

And the afterlife? Is the hope of eternal life for animals a mere wish of the gentle-hearted people who love them? Or can that hope be really realistically realized? The apostle Paul may want to weigh in on that. He frequently uses the Greek word *elpis* in his writings, translated as *hope*, referring to God's promises, in the fulfillment of which we can have absolute assurance. On the topic of justification by faith, Paul states plainly in Romans 5:5, "hope does not disappoint us . . . ." So we may rightfully inquire, "Will that confidence extend to Romans 8:19–21?"

> *The creation waits in eager expectation for the sons of God to be revealed. For the creation was subjected to frustration, not by its own choice, but by the will of the one who subjected it, in hope that the creation itself will be liberated from its bondage to decay and brought into the glorious freedom of the children of God.*

Acknowledgments

Therefore encourage one another and build each other up . . .

—1 THESSALONIANS 5:11

THE BACKGROUND RESEARCH FOR this book was started at Southern Illinois University years ago, and to this day, I value the encouragement given by colleagues in the history department as well as at Morris Library.

Continual appreciation cannot adequately express my thanks to Dr. John S. Haller who took time to be my mentor in spite of his responsibilities as academic vice-president of the university. He was not only tremendously knowledgeable and insightful, but also personally kind, optimistic, and inspiring. It is no secret that we are not on the same page spiritually—he an atheist, I a Christian—but he always exhibited respect for my position and never attempted to persuade me otherwise. It is true that this present volume is more overtly Christian than its predecessor, and I realize that it may give Dr. Haller an additional gray hair or two. Hopefully no more than that!

Special thanks are also owed to Dr. James Smith Allen who was always willing to listen to and engage with my peculiar ideas, as well as to share with me his stimulating research on nineteenth-century France, which I enjoyed tremendously.

For the reader's pleasure, I encourage you to seek out the books that both of these professors have written: John Haller's, primarily on medical history, education, and Swedenborgianism, and Jim Allen's on *l'histoire de la belle France*. All are fascinating.

Further acknowledgments include my good friend and enthusiastic motivator Doug Douma, founder of SOLA Appalachian Trail ministry, pastor of Unionville Bible Presbyterian Church (New York), and author of *The Presbyterian Philosopher: Biography of Gordon H. Clark* (the first page of which is the dedication to Doug's absolutely wonderful dog *Henry*, and the last page of the index concluding with *Zephi*, Gordon Clark's beloved dachshund). I give thanks also to Tim Taylor, director of the Newman Center at Southern Illinois University, who graciously read this manuscript to make sure I had correctly represented Roman Catholic doctrine and Aristotelian philosophy; my compassionate neighbor, Emily Hartmann, who lovingly rescues turtles, snakes, Luna moths, and any animal in distress, no matter the situation; my friend and encourager Pam Vaughan-Knaus, Colorado State University honors program senior instructor; Anne Ruolt, mon amie et professeur à l'Institut Biblique de Nogent-sur-Marne; and many folks at Grace Presbyterian Church, Carbondale, IL, who have amiably accepted my oddities.

I am also indebted to the Revd. Dr. Robin Parry, theologian, philosopher, Anglican priest, and author of several fascinating books, also graciously serving as editor of this book. Not only has he taken the time to answer my many questions, but also to converse about the history of England—particularly Stonehenge!

And finally, infinite thanks go to my family: four terrific sons (Seth, Nathan, Luke, and Benjamin) who have loved our furry, finned, and feathered friends in house and woods, and my incredibly patient husband Wyatt, who has put up with me for fifty-five years, encouraged me every step of the way, and always kept calm when I grumbled and crumbled over my own incompetence, technological and otherwise! Without him, this book would not exist.

Abbreviations

ISBE	*International Standard Bible Encyclopedia*
JETS	*Journal of the Evangelical Theological Society*
NIV	*New International Version*
NYSJM	*New York State Journal of Medicine*
NIDCC	*New International Dictionary of the Christian Church*
PSM	*Popular Science Monthly*

A Fur-Ever Future?

Let every creature praise his holy name for ever and ever.

—PSALM 145:21

WHEN NATURALIST JANE GOODALL handed Vicki the chimp a stack of photographs and asked her to separate them into two piles—pictures of humans and pictures of chimps—Vicki was equal to the task. Confidently she separated the pictures. Her only "mistake" was putting the photo of herself in the human pile! Apparently, Vicki believed that the essential difference between humans and non-humans is *not* bodily structure. But what that essential difference is remains a question that philosophers, theologians, humanitarians, and even historians continue to debate, with the ebb and flow of intensity that normally inheres in any curious metaphysical issue. The problem of defining "human" and "non-human" is not, however, a matter of mere curiosity. It is a topic of fundamental importance, touching the very essence of life. What is human? What is animal? Vicki may know the answer!

When the topic of a book is animals, readers might assume that it was written by a veterinarian, a vegetarian, or, better yet, a

Dr. Seuss! When the topic is immortality, the author should be a philosopher or a theologian. Put the two together in the framework of historical research and some people sniff, "Sentimentality," while secularists sigh and Christians cry, "Heresy!" So to be able to articulate anything more profound than mono-verbal sputterings, research is in order.

Research into the history of thought pertaining to the immortality of animals is readily available and always stimulating. In our contemporary world, however, belief in an afterlife even for human beings is often considered the epitome of naïveté, and for animals an absurdity. Although Buddhists still expect to be gathered into the ultimate world-soul and the majority of Christians still affirm the truth of heaven (for humans only), materialistic science and the high-tech culture of Western society have nearly excluded serious consideration of spiritual reality not only from the academic realm but from the minds of the general populace. Consequently, to write or to read a history of belief in animal immortality might appear to be an exercise in futility.

Modern Concern for Animals

Fortunately, to be sure, it is undeniable and encouraging that there is a marked increase of interest in the environment as a whole and in the welfare of animals, both domesticated and wild. Credit certainly is due to two well-known authors who pioneered in-depth research and bravely exposed some of the worst environmental issues of the twentieth century. Rachel Carson's *Silent Spring* (1962) alerted the world to the disasters of using chemicals to control "pests," and Peter Singer's *Animal Liberation* (1975) shocked thoughtful readers as he unveiled the horrors of the treatment of animals in scientific experimentation and in food industries and called for complete changes in practice and profound revisions of ethical codes. Their work—and that of those who have followed in their footsteps—has borne fruit.

Within the Christian world, for example, Tony Campolo, pastor, professor, and author, shows clearly in *How to Rescue the Earth without Worshiping Nature* (1992) that it is truly the Christian's responsibility to care for the environment, to be alert and active, and take steps to eradicate the suffering of animals. R. C. Sproul, founder of Ligonier Ministries, has made the point that animals (and other elements of nature) obey "the laws of nature, which in fact are the laws of God. There's no disobedience." He contrasts this to human beings who "practice the persistent type of disobedience for which we are known," a consequence of which is that animals suffer *innocently*.[1]

Another proponent of animal care, in a comprehensive, academic, respected, and enjoyably readable tome, philosopher Stephen Webb authored *On God and Dogs: A Christian Theology of Compassion for Animals*. Curiously, after explaining the viewpoints of many noted philosophers, scientists, and theologians pertaining to the compassionate treatment of animals, Webb observes that although animal afterlife is a topic that "many people like to discuss . . . theologians find it unnerving."[2]

One theologian who has virtually dissected the issue of the suffering of animals and of their possible immortality is Christopher Southgate of Exeter University. In his analyses of the problems in the interweaving of Christianity and evolution, he faces the frustrating matter of reconciling the reality of a loving Creator-God with the reality of agony and evil in the world. As theologian, philosopher, and scientist, Southgate offers a thorough discussion of the dilemma, as well as suggestions for in-depth, long-term, and world-wide contemporary measures to help alleviate the pain of the natural world.[3]

As for progress in contemporary western culture, as noted above, interest in the welfare of animals, both domesticated and wild, is increasing. We care about animals. For instance, many "sanctuaries" for helpless animals have been established, one excellent example of which is Mission: Wolf, located near Westcliffe, Colorado, where helpless wolves and horses are protected while

1. Sproul, *Now That's a Good Question*, 166–67.

2. Webb, *On God and Dogs*, 174.

3. Southgate, *The Groaning of Creation*.

being permitted to remain as wild as they wish.[4] Wolves who show more affinity toward humans are trained to educate visitors; it is a wonderful experience to receive a gentle kiss from a wolf, as I can personally attest, having been kissed by one who responds to her name, Soleil.[5] The most congenial wolves also go on school tours all over the United States, presenting their unique intelligence and beautiful personalities to amazed audiences.

Our concern for and interest in animals is further exemplified, for instance, by the fact that the American legal system provides protection for animals,[6] environmentalists work hard to try to preserve natural habitats, and shelters constantly search for "Furever Homes" for their little orphans. Many animals show evidence of ability to reason, can be trained to be companions for senior citizens or victims of various sorts of trauma, and seem to understand how to help in a wide variety of situations. Intelligent dogs serve extremely well in police work and in the military, and certainly deserve their military honors. Articles, magazines, and books about animals continue to be written, new kinds of dog and cat food promise better health, and farm stores suddenly sell out of sunflower seed for the birds when the temperature heads toward sub-zero and the snow is deep! Improving life for animals seems to be popular these days and it is increasingly easy to find books about animal needs, personalities, fair treatment worldwide, and so on. Given such interest in the lives of animals here and now, is it pointless to ask about their potential for life in the hereafter?

4. Brooks, *A Walk in Connection* is a delightful book, authored by the wife of the director of Mission: Wolf, Kent Weber, whose understanding of the wolves is truly impressive.

5. A person who undoubtedly meant well had tried to raise this wolf as a dog; disappointed, he turned the wolf over to our son Luke, who named her Soleil (Sunshine!) and took her to Mission: Wolf.

6. As one example, note the rescue of hundreds of beagle pups from a puppy mill in Virginia, reported on by ABC News on August 25, 2022.

Some Words about Words

Two key words

The very word "animal" can lead to serious discussion of future life (i.e. immortality) since it comes from the Latin *animalis*, itself derived from *anima*, meaning "breath" or "soul." Animals, in other words, were so named because they are beings with the breath of life, or "soul." "Animal" then gives us other words such as animism (vitality) and animated (lively) while its original meaning (soul) can easily lead to the use of related terms that are crucial in reflecting on the topic at hand. These may include "spirit," "personality," "consciousness," "immortality," "eternity," even "life" itself. What is life? Is it *anima*? Is it an immaterial, indestructible reality that will endure forever? Or is it a collection of particles that will disintegrate, decay, and disappear?

Is immortality the feature that separates human from non-human? What about the soul? Is it the *anima*? This book attempts to grapple with these issues and encourages the reader to do so, too.

The word "image" is also of great importance as we look at immortality; however, it does not derive from *anima* but from *imago*. There is a definite difference in the meanings, implications, and interpretations of the *imago Dei*, the "image of God," so much so as to warrant a book of its own. Suffice it to say here that in Genesis 1, the "image" is attributed to humans only and will be mentioned briefly in the final chapter.

A warning about changing meanings

A problem that arises all too often when considering comprehensible vocabulary is when words change meaning over the course of time, probably because of cultural developments. Take for example the word "end." Nowadays it means the conclusion or finality of an event or position (as the "end of the line"). Formerly it referred to the "purpose" or "goal" of an action or event and is so used in various quotations within this book.

Animal Afterlife?

As far as the "animal" itself is concerned, the frequently used word "brute" in historic quotations should not be understood disrespectfully; it formerly just meant "non-human" or "without ability to reason." It did not mean savage, crude, insensitive, violent, or brutal, as it does today. So when reading the works of authors of the past, it is important to remember that when they refer to "the brutes" they are simply referring to animals in contrast to humans.

Moving Forward

In view of tenuous vocabulary and the need for earthly compassion for animals, is the consideration of animal *afterlife* absurd? Many environmentalists might think so. So do many Christians. Granted, the "here and now" is indeed vitally important. But so is an understanding of life after death, and some people are certainly willing to talk about it. It is not futile to check out what has been written in the past and to reflect on one's own opinions of the matter. Discussions between people even of opposing viewpoints can lead to mutual benefit—for both human and animal. This book attempts to present a variety of opinions, while maintaining its conclusion from the position of belief in biblical truth and reformed theology.

Irrespective of the conclusions we might reach regarding an animal afterlife, there is still much we can learn—even about God—from animals. As Job says, "ask the animals, and they will teach you." They know that "the life of every creature and the breath of all mankind" are in the Lord's hand (Job 12:7–10). To God be all glory! *Furever.*

—— **2** ——

Defining Definitions

Find out . . . and come back to me with definite information.

—1 SAMUEL 23:23

Definite Information?

DEFINITIONS? HOW OFTEN WORDS defy definite definition! Yet they must be defined, mustn't they! Alas, the task is not always easy. The words that lie at the heart of this book have been, and continue to be, defined in various ways, causing confusion, evoking a variety of responses, and providing conversation, sometimes enjoyable and sometimes fractious! So—

Afterlife. Immortality. Nirvana. Transmigration. State of consciousness. Eternal life. Most of these terms would require the existence of a "soul," but what is a "soul"? Authors, past and present, have grappled with that problem. In the brief conceptual overview that follows, do you agree with, or like, any of these? Choose as you wish!:

Animal Afterlife?

Moses:	life-breath, an individual living person
Socrates:	manifestation of the idea of life
Plato:	self-initiating motion
Aristotle:	organizing principle of life: sensitive, nutritive, and/or rational
St. Augustine:	immortal moral agent
Thomas Aquinas:	rationality
Descartes:	non-material mental substance characterized by thought
Pierre Bayle:	a substance that thinks
MJP Flourens:	instinct
Boucher de Perthes:	conscience, moral sense, memory
Arthur Mangin:	divine breath
Ralph W. Emerson:	infinite ocean of life
Charles Hodge:	animating principle of the body (spirit, mind, heart, self)
E. Marais:	psyche, conscience, moral understanding
P. Prewitt:	emotions and reason
G. Kowalski:	marrow of existence as sentient, sensitive beings; the magic of life
Mary Buddemeyer	the essence of life, the person him- or herself
Sy Montgomery	no definite definition, but a comprehensive list of possibilities![1]

The topic of animal immortality is very rambling indeed, inasmuch as there are so many perceptions of the "soul." Perusing

1. These authors and the works that specified their definitions are as follows: Moses is found in the Torah; Socrates and Plato in Plato's *Phaedo*, discussed in Bevan, *Genesis*, 153–57; Aristotle in Copleston, *History of Philosophy*, 232–34, 71–73; Descartes in Rosenfield, *Beast-Machine*, 21, 47; Augustine in Humphry, Almond, Armitage. The others are included by name in the bibliography at the end of this book.

through history, it can become frustrating to realize how many definitions have been proposed, accepted, rejected, reaffirmed, tweaked, discarded, merged, mixed, melded—and used with great authority to build religious, scientific, or philosophical systems. Perhaps this book should be entitled "Animal Afterlife: Discombobulated Developments Depicted."

To forestall that bleak dilemma, however, the discussion presented in this historical account will involve four explanations which, after centuries of debate, became accepted by those who have cared about philosophical and theological accuracy pertaining to animals and their ultimate destiny. In brief, these are 1) sensation, 2) intelligence, 3) moral sense, 4) spirit.

Soul as Sensation

The great Greek philosopher Aristotle attempted to understand and to explain the soul as the principle of life itself. Living things, souls, could be nutritive (plants, animals, humans), sensitive (animals and humans), and/or rational (humans). By "sensation," Aristotle speaks of the source of knowledge acquired via the living bodily senses of sight, sound, smell, taste, and touch. He granted this type of soul to both humans and animals, but added the element of rationality for humans, thus distinguishing them from animals. And since sensory perception could be attained only by a living body, the sensitive soul existed for this life only.

Pursuing Aristotelian philosophy in the late Middle Ages, Thomas Aquinas (1225–74) agreed that knowledge comes via the senses and that because animals have eyes, ears, etc., they have a living sensitive soul, but they are not living rational souls. In his explanation of creation, he wrote, "For as birds and fishes have a living soul, so also have land animals. But these animals are not themselves living souls."[2] For animals, then, sense perception is the full extent of the function of a soul.

2. Aquinas, *Summa Theologiae*, Treatise on the Work of the Six Days, Question 72: On the Work of the Sixth Day.

Several centuries later, the scientist René Descartes (1596-1650) weighed in on the idea of a sensate soul in animals. However, he went a lot further than either Aristotle or Aquinas. Explaining "sensation" as being aware of one's surroundings and situations, he believed that animals have no self-awareness, no self-identity, and thus no awareness, even of pain. He saw them simply as beings that function *like machines*, moving, responding, but only mechanically—behaving *as if* they are aware, yet *not* actually aware. His ideas have not been widely accepted, though recognized as a "scientific" basis for developments in some modern industries (e.g., puppy mills or meat production), which many pro-animal organizations are currently addressing.

Soul as Intelligence

Granting that animals have a soul that functions as long as the body functions, but that they are not actually a rational soul, Aquinas had proceeded to identify rationality and free will as elements of the intellect, "incorporeal and subsistent."[3] This was crucial in distinguishing human from animal, for, according to Aquinas, with intelligence, humans are immortal, but without it, the animal is not *in its essence* a soul, and therefore not immortal.

However, another philosopher, of Huguenot parentage, Pierre Bayle (1647–1706), became the animals' defender and launched a debate opposing both Aquinas and Descartes. He wrote that it should be "clear to all intelligent persons that a thing which feels, knows that it feels." "It is no more absurd to deny that a man's soul actually knows what it perceives through the senses than to deny that a dog knows it sees a bird when it sees one."[4] Bayle says of the soul of the animal, "it is therefore a substance that thinks; it is therefore capable of thought in general; it can therefore receive all sorts of thoughts; therefore it is able to reason . . . ."[5] In effect, the soul

3 Aquinas, *Summa Theologiae*, Question 75, Article 2.

4. Bayle, quoted in Hastings, *Man and Beast*, 24.

5. Bayle, quoted in Hastings, *Man and Beast*, 25, from *Dictionnaire Historique* (1740), IV, 79. The original reads: "elle est donc une substance qui pense,

of beast is equal to the soul of man in its incipient intelligence and differs only by "an accidental difference due to something external, to physical organs."[6] Bayle concluded therefore that the animal's rational soul is only a little less competent intellectually than that of the human being.

Yet another French philosopher, Jacques Boucher de Perthes (1788–1868), furthered the discussion by focusing on five particular considerations that strengthened the argument for animal intelligence: 1) animal instinct and human intelligence are absolutely identical; 2) human soul and animal soul are of one principle, and differ only in degree; 3) animal soul has not developed sufficiently to be divided into spirit, reason, and talent (if it could, animals would be human); 4) animal soul can grow, expand, and improve; 5) animals improve in the same manner as human beings—by study, will, experience, and reflection.[7] These points, however, opened a debate involving not only intelligence—but morality as well.

Soul as Moral Sense

An objector to the idea of animal intelligence was J. C. Prichard (1786–1848), a British physician who specialized in studies of the mind. He, and others, posited that the essence of personhood is more than intelligence, and began the search for evidence of the soul as manifested, not by mere intelligence but by volition and moral sense, which in turn produces intentional behavior, and necessitates the property of memory, attributable in Prichard's view solely to human beings.

Those who already believed in the intelligence of animals objected strenuously to such a restriction of memory, and popular anecdotal books at that time recorded many instances of long-term memory in animals. One such report is of a stray mongrel dog whose broken leg was set by a kind veterinarian. When healed,

---

elle est donc capable de la pensée en général: elle peut donc recevoir toutes sortes de pensées, elle peut donc raisonner . . . ."

6. Hastings, *Man and Beast*, 25.

7. Boucher de Perthes, *De la Création*.

the dog disappeared, but returned eight months later—bringing with him another dog whose leg was broken![8] Memory of location, event, and result all figured in this dog's action, as well as anticipation of a repeated procedure, and that not even for his own benefit.

Boucher de Perthes insisted that recognition of animal intelligence necessitates recognition of the possession of memory, which he believed to be a quality of living beings.[9] On the foundation of memory, conscience develops, and from the conscience moral vice or virtue derive. In some cases, anecdotes extended the moral sense even beyond justice and generosity. The story was told of a man who tried to drown his dog in the Seine River by repeatedly pushing it overboard. At last the boat capsized and the man who could not swim would have drowned had not the dog itself rescued him. Reflecting on this incident, a local pastor asked a simple question, yet one with profound ramifications: "Was not this dog morally superior to his owner, in thus returning good for evil?"[10]

Soul as Spirit

The idea of the soul as an immortal spirit appears in both Christian and non-Christian literature, with some contrasting explanations.

Throughout the Scriptures of the Old and New Testaments, the idea of the soul, not only as immortal, but also as personal, is foundational. This soul bears responsibility in this life on earth and continues its existence and awareness of its own condition and surroundings after the death of the body. Believers in the Judeo-Christian God—in spite of differences in theology and practice—have usually acknowledged the immortality of the individual human soul.

---

8. Morris, *Records of Animal Sagacity*, 40.

9. Boucher de Perthes, *De la Création*, Book IV, 1–2. He seems to have believed that plants were intelligent. He wrote "If plants are alive, it is necessary that they have a will (or volition) of their own." (Vol. III, 407; translation mine). The "intelligence" of plants, understood in a suitably nuanced way, is an issue that has marked some recent scientific work on them.

10. Morris, *Records of Animal Sagacity*, 75.

The soul as immortal, but *impersonal*, can be found in various ancient eastern religions and philosophies. This concept came most visibly into western thought in the nineteenth century as Europeans and Americans became increasingly interested in eastern ideas.

The fascination of a universal spirit, of reincarnation, and of a Buddhist Nirvana captured the minds of some rather outstanding intellectuals. Well-known individuals—Ralph Waldo Emerson and Bronson Alcott, among others—had become disaffected with the direction of rationalistic philosophy and traditional Christianity and fell in love with the beauty and mystique of the Orient. A group of such thinkers organized the Transcendentalist Club, of which Emerson became the primary spokesman. He believed that our earthly destiny unfolds in Nature because "we rest as the earth lies in the soft arms of the atmosphere; that Unity, that Over-Soul, within which every man's particular being is contained and made one with all others. . . . [W]ithin man is the soul of the whole, . . . the universal beauty, . . . the eternal ONE." In an ecstasy of worship, Emerson could rhapsodize, "I, the imperfect, adore my own Perfect. . . . More and more the surges of everlasting nature enter into me. . . . So come I to live in thoughts and act with energies which are immortal."[11]

Transcendentalism and Buddhism (as well as another system known as Theosophy) are connected, and all found their adherents in nineteenth-century Europe and America. They believed that for animal and human alike, the soul is immortal, but is not itself distinct. There is no expectation of any *individual* conscious personality in future existence, for all individuals will have evaporated into a nebulous empyrean.

Conclusion

Concepts? Definitions? Descriptions? Throughout the centuries of curiosity and conversation about the origin—or even the existence—of the soul, people have had to attempt to settle

11. Emerson, "The Over-Soul," in *The Complete Essays*, 261–78.

on explanations that are mutually agreeable. Christian or non-Christian, the issue can be perplexing enough when discussing the human soul, and when it extends to an immortal, personal animal soul, it becomes even more so! Ideas, evaluations, and interpretations viewed through the lens of western history are truly fascinating.

For this particular study, organizationally and historically, the Bible is the place to begin, not only because of its ancient authorship, but also because it does address the relevance of the natural world in relationship to humanity. A Christian view of animal life, present and future, must ultimately derive from God's Word.

It is also important to understand non-biblical ideas inasmuch as they have wide and deep impact in the worlds of thought and action—past, present, and future. It has been my intention to consider the most important of these ideas and to evaluate their strengths and weaknesses.

Ideas, evaluations, and interpretations viewed through the lens of western history can certainly be fascinating, frustrating, or fulfilling—depending on your definitions!

3

Torah and Talmud

In the beginning, God created the heavens and the earth.

—GENESIS 1:1

Almighty Creator

eternal Essence, omnipresent—
Triune
power
glory.

unchanging Thought, omniscient—
Plan
wisdom
truth.

divine Movement, omnipotent—
Hovering
speaking
fulfilling.

Hebrew Scripture: Old Testament

ACCORDING TO THE HEBREW Scripture, the Spirit of God "hovered over the waters," subsequently creating light, darkness, sky, ocean, land, vegetation, sun, moon, stars, great creatures of the sea, winged birds, wild animals, livestock, creatures that move along the ground, and human beings. It was a full world! Some time later, after the great flood, God established a covenant with humans (Noah and family)—*and* "with every living creature . . . the birds, the livestock, and all the wild animals"—promising not to destroy the earth with a flood ever again, the rainbow being designated as the sign that God will remember his "everlasting covenant" with *all living creatures of every kind on the earth.*" Can there possibly be any stronger evidence of the creational equality of human and non-human?

Torah and Beyond

Having begun with the account of God's creating the universe and pronouncing it all "very good,"[1] it was a basic assumption of Old Testament authors that a primary purpose of the natural world is to manifest God's glory. Moses used the phrase "as surely as the glory of the LORD fills the whole earth,"[2] Isaiah stated that "the whole earth is full of his glory,"[3] and Habakkuk wrote that God's "glory covered the heavens and his praise filled the earth."[4] The Psalmist provided an additional teleological statement when he wrote, "The heavens declare the glory of God; the skies proclaim the work of his hands."[5]

In the accounts of creation and the flood in the first several chapters of the Torah (i.e. the Pentateuch), the importance and value of animal life was affirmed, and throughout the remainder of the Hebraic Scripture similar affirmations appear relatively

1. Genesis 1:9, 25, 31.
2. Numbers 14:21.
3. Isaiah 6:3.
4. Habakkuk 3:3.
5. Psalm 19:1.

frequently. There is scarcely a page of Scripture that does not refer in some way to the natural world. References to clouds, mountains, plains, valleys, rivers, rain, crops, and animals—both wild and domesticated—are practically innumerable. Of course, one cannot deny that many citations are allegories, similes, or metaphors, but also that garnishing the context with imaginative comparisons enriches the artistry of these ancient volumes and prompts the reader to reflect more deeply on God's intentions. When the patriarch Jacob blessed his son Issachar as a "rawboned donkey" in a pleasant land, this is not the same sort of language as Saul's when he went to look for his father's lost donkeys in the hill country of Ephraim.[6] Or consider the lions. The devil "prowls around like a roaring lion!" Not the same lions who were in the den with Daniel! Later, because of human violence, the prophet wrote that "the land mourns," while in better times "the lands are at rest and at peace."[7]

It is perfectly obvious that while some passages are allegorical, many, such as Saul's donkeys and Daniel's lions, refer to actual animals in the visible, tangible world.[8] The author of Psalms 105 and 106 certainly had real historical fish, frogs, flies, and gnats in mind when he recounted the famous plagues in Egypt and a real wasteland through which the Israelites passed on their way to Canaan.[9] Further, inasmuch as ancient Israel was a rural society, the recipients of the writings could identify with pastoral, agrarian, and topographical descriptions. When the writer of the book of Joshua stated that the Jordan River is "at flood stage all during

6. Genesis 49:14; 1 Samuel 9:3.

7. Hosea 4:3; Isaiah 14:7.

8. A note about the interpretation of Scripture or of exegesis: the historical/grammatical approach has proved reliable as opposed to mere literalism, allegorical, or mythological, etc., approaches. The point is simply that biblical authors wrote according to their ability to use language in all of its literary variation while the Spirit of God worked in them to write Truth. The reader thus tries to figure what was the intent in using the elements of form such as simile, metaphor, parallelism, et al., and can unfortunately make mistakes, while the biblical author certainly did not.

9. Psalms 105:29–41 and 106:14.

harvest," farmers understood the danger.[10] Similarly, military defeat on the plains of Megiddo and the aborted escape through the valley of Jericho might be blamed on geography.[11] Nor is a desert inhabited only by jackals, owls, and hyenas a particularly desirable environment for Hebrew shepherds![12] And when the Psalmist looked up to the mountains, asking rhetorically if he would receive any help from those rocky crags, he knew the answer.[13] Nature can be exceedingly hostile.

Nature can also be refreshing. The Israelites knew the blessings of the "precious dew from heaven above," the dependability of the rising sun, the spring and autumn rains, the fragrance of blossoming vines, and the cool shade of the forest trees.[14] The great King Solomon apparently had a passion for biology, for he "described plant life, from the cedar of Lebanon to the hyssop that grows out of walls" and "taught about animals and birds, reptiles and fish." Wise men of "all nations" came to learn from this Hebrew king.[15]

Donkeys, lions, insects, landscapes, and many other things comprise nature, and Yahweh-God, the Creator of it all, "preserves both man and beast."[16] He reserves wilderness areas for wild animals and feeds the denizens of field, forest, and ocean.[17] Commands of care and protection are stipulated for the preservation of the wilderness and also to prevent hunting to extinction.[18] The Decalogue itself expresses the creational equality of human and animal by providing one day of rest in every seven for one's son, daughter, man-servant, maid-servant, alien, *and animal*.[19] Furthermore, Yahweh insists that animals who labor for the benefit

10. Joshua 3:15.

11. 2 Chronicles 35:22; 2 Kings 25:4–5.

12. Isaiah 34:13–14.

13. Psalm 121:1.

14. Deuteronomy 33:13; Hosea 6:3; Song of Solomon 2:3, 13.

15. 1 Kings 4:33–34.

16. Psalm 36:6.

17. Psalms 104:10–28 and 147:8–9.

18. Deuteronomy 22:6–7 and Psalm 104:18.

19. Exodus 20:10 and 23:10–12.

of mankind must be given good working conditions, specifically that they be permitted to eat at will and that they be comfortable.[20] Owners are to provide all that their animals need; and if a person finds even an unknown animal injured or straying, he is to care for the creature until its owner is located.[21] It is interesting that even in spiritual matters, there is an example of Yahweh's love for animals: when the prophet Jonah was disgusted with his assignment in Nineveh (even though both man and beast had put on the sackcloth of repentance), God rebuked him by pointing out that he, God, was concerned, not only about the hundred and twenty thousand children in that great city, but about the *cattle* as well.[22]

The breadth of Jehovah's interest shown to non-human creatures in this tangible world raises the question of whether he shows any concern for them beyond the grave. They certainly appear in prophetic passages such as the famous "peaceable kingdom" descriptions in Isaiah 11 and 65 where animals are the primary actors. In a future state, lions will eat straw with oxen and lambs while wolves, leopards, goats, calves, cows, bears, cobras, vipers, and children will all play together.[23] Visionary passages frequently offer two or more possible fulfillments for a given picture. To interpret the Isaiah prophecies as a time of earthly social justice or as a beatific millennium could be acceptable, but to eliminate an eternal consideration would be too constrictive. Zechariah 2:4, whatever the interpretation of it may be, clearly includes animals and human beings *equally* in a *future* Jerusalem. God does *not* omit animals in the Old Testament prophecies of the age to come.

Talmud and Beyond

Hebrew thought and culture rest not only on the Old Testament but also on the Talmud, which is a summary of oral law developed

---

20. Deuteronomy 25:4 and 22:10.

21. Deuteronomy 22:1–4.

22. Jonah 4:11.

23. Isaiah 11:6–8 and 65:25.

between the close of the Old Testament and the beginning of the Middle Ages. As a "conglomerate of law, legend, and philosophy, a blend of unique logic and shrewd pragmatism, of history and science, anecdotes and humor," it speaks to both theoretical and practical issues. Its major purpose is to point the Jewish people to the "positive religious duty of studying Torah," and to know how to apply its teachings to their lives.[24] In an agrarian world, it was imperative to know the proper relationship of human and animal; and where the Mosaic injunctions seemed incomplete, rabbis spelled out details and explanations in the Talmud. In some cases this led to a study of animal anatomy and physiology. The Talmudic authors were not always in agreement as to whether the banning of eating certain parts of an animal was for reasons of health or sacrifice, but all agreed that the command not to eat blood was clear: "be sure you do not eat the blood, *because the blood is the life, and you must not eat the life with the meat.*"[25]

Whether the equivalence of blood and life is parallel to the concept of soul and immortality is a point of debate. One line of reasoning is that by combining Genesis 9:4–6 with Deuteronomy 12:20–28, the equal value of both human and non-human blood in the sight of God is established.[26] Non-human blood had to be offered to God, an *equivalent* of the "accounting" for the life of a human being. An Italian author at the turn of the twentieth century, Countess Evelyn Martinengo Cesaresco (1852–1931), concluded that "Jews believed every animal had a soul, a spirit, which was beyond human jurisdiction, with which they had no right to tamper" and that "the soul—whatever it was—appeared to the Jews to possess one nature whether in men or in animals."[27] The implication of such an idea is that if the human soul is destined for immortality, so is the animal's.

24. Steinsaltz, *Essential Talmud*, 4.

25. Deuteronomy 12:23.

26. A nineteenth-century commentator, Adam Clarke (1762–1832), wrote of Genesis 9:5, "This is very obscure, but if taken literally it seems to be an awful warning against cruelty to the brute creation." Clarke, *Commentary on the Bible*, Abridged by R. Earle, 31.

27. Cesaresco, *Open Court*, Vol. XV.

Further thoughts pertaining to animals appear in Jewish books known as the Enoch literature. One idea is purely allegorical: biblical characters are represented by animals. But the Second Book of Enoch reveals deeper considerations and comparisons of the souls of human and animal, asserting that "the Lord will not judge a single animal soul for the sake of man; but human souls he will judge for the sake of the souls of their animals. In the great Age there is a special place for human beings. And just as every human soul is according to number, so also it is with animal souls. And not a single soul which the Lord has created will perish until the great judgment. And every kind of animal soul will accuse the human beings who have fed them badly."[28] What is expected after the "great judgment" is not specified, but it would seem at least that mankind bears responsibility for treating animals well, in view of judgment and future life.

In *Animal Life in Jewish Tradition: Attitudes and Relationships*, E. J. Schochet, professor at the Academy of Jewish Religion in New York, explores other eschatological possibilities. Schochet perceives the Bible as *demythologizing* animals by casting them as part of the natural background for human action or giving them a utilitarian function. *Remythologizing* the animals fell to the rabbis, whose oral and written literature included not only allegories in which animals serve to symbolize other things, but fairy-tale-like stories of exotic creatures who went through fantastic metamorphoses and performed extraordinary feats.[29] Two biblical animals, Leviathan and Behemoth, appear in the hereafter, but only briefly, inasmuch as their flesh comprises "the menu for a sumptuous feast" and their hide will be "spread as a luminous canopy around the walls of Jerusalem"![30] In a series of lectures entitled *The Hereafter in Jewish and Christian Thought*, the Anglican bishop C. V. Pilcher (1879–1961) notes the presence and demise only of Leviathan in the restored Garden of Eden; he alludes to no other animals in Hebrew eschatology. Schochet credits two medieval rabbinical

28. 2 Enoch 58:6–7; translation by F. Andersen.
29. Schochet, *Animal Life*, 84–94.
30. Schochet, *Animal Life*, 85.

groups (the Karaites and the Mutazilites) with attributing an afterlife of reward and compensation for all animals who have suffered on earth but recognizes that their teachings were rejected.[31] Schochet's conclusion is the opposite of the Italian countess. He believes that in the Jewish tradition "man's spiritual development entails a lonely climb to the summit."[32]

The Old Testament in some of its later texts[33] and the Talmud affirm Hebrew belief in life after death. King David's confidence in eternal bliss rings clear with such statements as "God shall redeem my soul from the power of the grave; for he shall receive me," and "Thou shalt guide me with thy counsel, and afterward receive me into glory."[34] The Talmud declares that "This world is a road-side inn, but the world to come is a real home," and "To the world of future bliss, like a vestibule is this. In the vestibule prepare for life eternal."[35]

Scripture: New Testament

In the New Testament, the apostle Paul (a very well-educated Jew) explained that the natural world clearly reveals the "eternal power and divine nature" of God.[36] Thus, in accordance with the Torah, the purpose of the material creation is two-fold: to give glory to God and to reveal God to humankind.

The New Testament's direct references to animals are few—the Gadarene swine, the sparrows worth a farthing, the ox treading out the grain, the camel passing through the eye of the needle, plus some sheep, fish, roosters, and moths—and have been dissected almost like laboratory specimens. A principle that has frequently been overlooked, however, is that in Christian doctrine the Old

31. Schochet, *Animal Life*, 208 and 215.

32. Schochet, *Animal Life*, 300.

33. E.g., Dan 12:2; Isa 26; Pss 16; 17:15; 49:15; 73:24 and Job 19:25ff.

34. Psalm 49:15 and Psalm 73:24.

35. Peters, *Hebrew Hopes of Heaven*, 24.

36. Romans 1:20.

and New Testaments form one single and complete revelation; it is not necessary for Old Testament concepts to be repeated in order to remain true. Old Testament statements of God's preservation of animals, his commands to humans to care for and protect them, and their inclusion in the covenants are all foundational for New Testament statements pertaining to the natural world. New Testament references thus serve either as additional information to the Old or in very specific cases (animal sacrifice, for example) as deliberate change. The paucity of animal references in the New Testament does not imply absence of concern. If anything, Christ's teachings on the attribute of mercy in human affairs imply a broadening of responsibility toward animals.[37] And when the apostle Paul recounted, from the Old Testament, God's concern for the ox who is treading out the grain, he did not discard mercy for the animal, but applied the teaching for the benefit of human beings as well.[38]

Furthermore, the New Testament offers striking panoramas of the future life and activity of animals in three passages. First, in Romans 8:21 Paul states clearly that "the creation itself will be liberated from its bondage to decay and brought into the glorious freedom of the children of God."[39] Christian believers have always looked forward to an eternal glorious freedom, exempt from sin, sickness, and death; and, according to Paul, this same freedom awaits *whole* of creation, which includes the animals. This is eternal life, not annihilation!

The second passage to consider is 1 Corinthians 15:35–44, which teaches the resurrection of the glorified human body, different from the present body, and makes a tantalizing comparison with the variety of bodies of animals, fish, and birds in the present world. The obvious thrust of the passage is directed toward human beings, but it is of interest for this study that animals are included in the context of eternity, i.e. verses 42–43.

37. Matthew 5:7; 23:23; Luke 6:36; Hebrews 2:17; James 2:13.
38. Deuteronomy 25:4 and 1 Corinthians 9:9–10.
39. Romans 8:21.

The third reference is an extended prophetic view of heaven in the apostle John's Apocalypse that encompasses all animals, as John records that after the angels, the "four living creatures," and the elders had offered their praise to Christ, he heard "*every* creature in heaven and on earth and under the earth and on the sea, and all that is in them, singing . . . ."[40] The apparent conclusion of these verses, drawn from law, poetry, prophecy, and epistle, certainly suggests a future life for animals.

Hebrew Definitions

The concept of immortality or afterlife in almost any religious system presupposes some kind of immaterial essence. According to Christian theology, the immaterial element in humankind consists of the continuation of the thoughts and actions of individual consciousness after the death of the body.[41] For animals to exist in such an immortal state would require a similar invisible, conscious individuality. The common terms "soul" and "spirit" are loosely applied to designate the individual whose personal reality identifies him or her in life and continues after death, although the two words are frequently not interpreted as synonyms.

In the Old Testament there are two Hebrew words meaning "soul," both of which apply to human and non-human alike. The first word is *nephesh*, used in the sense of a living being, a creature with active, bodily expressions of life. This word appears in the first chapter of Genesis in the story of the creation of animals, who are referred to as "living *nepheshes*," and in the second chapter when, after God breathed the breath of life into the body, Adam became a "living *nephesh*." The breath of life that God breathed into the human body is *no different* from that which animates the non-human, since both become "*nepheshes*." Talmudic scholar Franz

40. Revelation 5:13.

41. The reunification of the immaterial element with the "glorified" body in the general resurrection at the return of Christ is a generally accepted Christian doctrine, except for "Christian materialists" who eliminate consciousness during the intermediate state.

Delitzsch (1813–90) believed that the *nephesh* constitutes the "self-living nature" of both man and beast and "may indicate not only the entire inner nature of man, but also his entire personality, i.e. all that pertains to the person of man."[42]

When there is no reference to a physical body, the other word for soul is used: *ruach* in Hebrew, connoting breath, wind, or ghost, and, according to the biblical scholar J. O. Buswell (1895–1982), it usually designates a non-material personal being.[43] In early Hebrew understanding, *ruach* and *nephesh* are identical in essence and origin, but different in function, the *nephesh* designating the "life principle" and the *ruach* signifying strong emotions.[44] By defining the *nephesh* and the *ruach* with these distinctions, one understood humanity to be a dichotomy, consisting of a body and a soul-spirit.

An opposing viewpoint explained by R. H. Charles (1855–1931), a scholar of Jewish literature, identified the "spirit" or "spirit of life" in an impersonal sense, never as "the bearer of the personality." Thus the spirit (impersonal life), common to man and the rest of the animal creation, animated the soul (personality); and at death when the spirit is withdrawn, the soul would be extinguished and all personal existence would cease.[45] This view necessitated a threefold division in individual essence (spirit, soul, and body) and was the basis for the rejection of belief in any immortality at all by the Jewish sect of Sadducees.[46] Charles asserted that this dissolution of the personality at death is recognized in Ecclesiastes 12:7, which states, "the dust returns to the ground it came from, and the spirit returns to God who gave it," meaning that the life force is simply re-absorbed into the "Supreme Fount of Life."[47] The author

---

42. Fallows, ed., *Popular and Critical Bible Encyclopaedia*, 1606. Quoted from Delitzsch, *Biblical Psychology*, 181–82.

43. Buswell, *Systematic Theology*, 240.

44. Charles, *Eschatology*, 45, 47.

45. Charles, *Eschatology*, 43–44.

46. Charles, *Eschatology*, 43.

47. Charles, *Eschatology*, 43. It is interesting to note that this idea appears again in some nineteenth-century sectarian explanations of the intermediate state.

of Ecclesiastes (whether Teacher, Preacher, Assembler, Qoheleth, or King Solomon) may have had some doubts about a future life, although his statement in 3:11 that God "has set eternity in the hearts of men" could indicate otherwise.[48] And the equality of the *ruach* of man and beast is the main point of the subsequent passage: "As for men, God tests them so that they may see that they are like the animals. . . . All have the same breath; man has no advantage over the animal. . . . Who knows if the spirit of man rises upward and if the spirit of the animal goes down into the earth?"[49] The purpose of this question about the destination of the spirit is to emphasize that the human is not superior to the animal. Without stretching the sense of the passage, it is clear that the author believed that the "adam" and the "behemoth" both have a *ruach*.

To attribute either *nephesh* or *ruach* exclusively to human beings, and to deny either one to non-humans, cannot be based on the Hebrew Scriptures. In fact, nowhere does the Scripture teach that animals do *not* have an immortal soul. The verses in Ecclesiastes, if interpreted cynically, could conceivably teach that neither man nor beast is blessed with immortality; but the author was not a philosophical or theological skeptic, but a Teacher whose message was to show that "neither wisdom nor pleasure could satisfy man's yearning for the enduring."[50] The Teacher concluded his message with an allusion to the spirit's returning to its Maker and an exhortation to prepare for the final judgment.

From Kingdom to Kingdom

During the reigns of David and Solomon, the Hebrew kingdom of Israel was among the mightiest on the face of the earth. Its military and economic power and influence stretched from the border of Egypt to the Euphrates River and from the Mediterranean Sea into the Eastern Desert. Militarily, David conquered all foreign rivals

---

48. Ecclesiastes 3:11.

49. Ecclesiastes 3:18–21.

50. Bullock, *Introduction to the Old Testament Poetic Books*, 194.

and established peace. Intellectually, the wise men of the world stood in awe of King Solomon. Economically, it was the pivot and thoroughfare of international commerce. Religiously, it stood for monotheism in a world of polytheists and continues to impact religious thought to this day. But kingdoms rise and fall; and in the subsequent centuries, Assyria, Babylonia, and Persia each enjoyed their moments of supreme splendor. At last, with twin victories at Salamis and Plataea, Greece brought down the Persian Empire and embarked on three centuries of nearly undisputed political power and twenty-five centuries of cultural influence in the western world. No matter what its destination may be, every intellectual highway in the West passes through Greece. Thus to continue probing ideas pertaining to animal immortality, we move from the Hebrew to the Greco-Roman world.

——— 4 ———

Greco-Roman Reasoning

I turned my mind to understand, to investigate and to
search out wisdom and the reason of things . . .

—ECCLESIASTES 7:25

. . . and knowledge will be pleasant to your soul.

—PROVERBS 2:10

Classical Questions

Before dealing with any idea of an *animal* soul, Greek and
Roman authors and philosophers, like people today, had to deal
with the very definition of "soul" and how it was or was not connected to the human body, whether or not it continued after death,
and how events in this life might impact one's potential future. Is it
any wonder that opinions and conclusions vary!

Homer, Hades, and Humanity?

Aided by gods, who were in fact very much like men, privileged ancient Greeks sought to achieve in a given lifetime the fullest possible development of individual natural abilities, whether military, political, academic, or literary. Exceptional achievers in any of these fields could possibly be made into demi-gods in the future life, but the vast majority of people expected to spend eternity in Hades, the abode of the dead "where flit the shades of worn-out men."[1] Only the very worst criminals would be sent to Tartarus. The traditional, or Homeric, concept of Hades, though not hell per se, was not a particularly happy place, and later Greeks sought a more beatific immortality. Orphic and Dionysian mystery religions attempted to construct a hopeful afterlife, and the Pythagoreans sought eternal salvation through knowledge.[2]

The Pythagoreans, best known for their geometry and intricate development of number theory, also taught the doctrine of metempsychosis, that is, the passing of the soul at death into another body. Certainly the idea of a soul with continued vigorous life after death was a pleasant contrast to Homer's shadowy future. However, although they taught that the soul is the "real" person, in their minds the soul could pass from human to human or from human to animal, unfettered by personal characteristics.

Socrates and Plato

For fuller definitions of the soul and an incipient idea of the soul's individuality, it is necessary to turn to the *Phaedo*, in which its author, Plato, uses the character of Socrates to explain his own ideas. There is debate about how much of the argument really comes from the historical Socrates and how much from Plato himself, but in any case, Plato deals well with the concepts of soul and immortality. In the conversation held on the day of his execution, Socrates affirmed that death is the separation of the soul from the

1. Clark, *Thales to Dewey*, 21.
2. Clark, *Thales to Dewey*, 22.

body, that the soul is immortal and divine, constituting the dominant principle in the human being, and that because the soul is the essence of *life*, it must be free from its contrary, *death*.[3] Plato further defined the soul as "self-initiating motion"; the soul, in other words, is not simply moved by forces outside itself, as a leaf blown by the wind is, but *moves itself*. It is, he believed, a particle of the divine mind and therefore immortal by nature. As superior to the body, the soul rules over it; intelligence is the crucial factor. "The only existing thing which properly possesses intelligence is soul," Plato asserted, "and this is an invisible thing, whereas fire, water, earth, and air are all visible bodies."[4] According to Plato, the embodied human soul consists of three parts—rational, spirited, and appetitive—of which the rational distinguishes man from animal and alone enjoys the privilege of immortality.[5] Therefore, since animals are not rational beings, Plato's understanding of afterlife (whatever that may be) has no animals. One possible exception or extension of this thought could be that if this afterlife is the realm of the *forms*, it could contain the *form* of *Dog*, say, though, of course, no individual dogs.

For Plato, "forms" were the timeless, spaceless universals—like beauty, goodness, and truth, and dog-ness—that, in his thought, are *more real* than particular, specific things—like a beautiful tree, a good ruler, a true promise, and Fido, my pet dog. To Plato, "[t]he real world, in contrast to the unreal world of perception, is composed of fixed, unchanging, absolute entities, called Forms or Ideas."[6] The rational soul contemplates specific things, like a particular cat, Felix, but it looks beyond the particular thing to the universals it participates in: the forms. If the climax of any afterlife is the realm of forms, it contains the singular form of dog or cat, but not any particular cats and dogs, like Felix and Fido.

3. Bevan, *Genesis and Evolution*, 153–57.

4. Copleston, *History*, 232.

5. Copleston, *History*, 234.

6. Clark, *Thales to Dewey*, 75.

Aristotle

Aristotle (384–22 B.C.) continued probing the nature and definition of the soul in his *De Anima*. Basically, he defined soul as the "principle of life," and, like Plato, he had a special priority for the *rational* capacity of the human soul, over the nutritive for plants and the nutritive and sensitive for animals. The distinctively human soul, the rational, is that which produces thought, and is signified by the Greek word *nous*, and can itself be divided into passive and active aspects. The passive *nous*, along with nutritive and sensitive souls, is inseparable from the body and perishes together with the body at physical death. Only the active *nous*, or active intellect, is immortal and eternal.[7]

Unfortunately, Aristotle was not able fully to define the active intellect, for it appears to be neither an individualized human mind nor an omniscient God. The lack of a definition for the active intellect gave rise to much subsequent discussion, including comprehensive writings by the esteemed Muslim scholar Averroes (Ibn Rushd, 1126–98) in which he offers theories of a "material intellect" and an "agent intellect" that can lead to universal knowledge. Twentieth-century philosopher Frederick Copleston (1907–94) has suggested further that Aristotle considered the active intellect as "a principle which is identical in all men, an Intelligence that has above it the hierarchy of the other separate Intelligence, that enters into man and functions within him, and that survives the death of the individual."[8] The *individualized* human soul, however, perishes. Interestingly, Aristotle noted that fellow-philosopher Anaxagoras (c. 430 B.C.) actually attributed intelligence to all animals, "both large and small, worthy and unworthy"; but Aristotle, by his concept of the "active intellect," considered intelligence and any sort of future existence for an animal far beyond the realm of possibility.[9]

An important exception to Aristotle's conclusion (six centuries later!) is evident in the writings of the Greek philosopher

---

7. Copleston, *History*, 71.

8. Copleston, *History*, 73.

9. Lovejoy and Boas, *Primitivism*, 389.

Plotinus (205–70) who took up the task of constructing an "integrated summation" of nearly a millennium of Greek wisdom. In his masterpiece, entitled *On the Immortality of the Soul*, he rejected Aristotle's theory of the soul and attacked Stoic materialism as well. Believing that the soul is "life" and that knowledge or "reminiscence" (integral to the soul) is eternal, Plotinus taught that the soul cannot die. Furthermore, since both the individual soul and the world-soul (i.e. the aggregation of all souls) are principles of motion, both are immortal. Thus Socrates, for example, is "just as immortal as the world-soul"; and on the same basis, Plotinus believed that the souls of animals and even plants are immortal.

Other Observations

One nineteenth-century pastor, Henry Harbaugh (1817–67), observed that belief in a future life was more widespread in the earlier centuries of Greco-Roman thought than in the "politer and more refined periods of pagan antiquity." As science and philosophy advanced, faith "hung in the doubtful, painful poise between hope and fear," and gradually declined.[10] And so in Greek thought, Harbaugh pointed out that Socrates (469–399 BC) anticipated joining "good men" in the afterlife, while in Roman thought, Cicero (106–43 BC) merely looked for a change of dwelling-place, Seneca (4–65 AD) expected extinction or possibly bliss, and Marcus Aurelius (121–80 AD) settled for annihilation.

The World of BC to AD

When in the course of human events, the Roman military power subdued and unified the Hellenistic world, Greek philosophy and Hebrew prophecy met quite unexpectedly. At the right time, as the Christian Scripture says, the Logos became flesh and made his dwelling among men.[11] Yahweh-Theos, in the person of the eternal

10. Harbaugh, *The Heavenly Home*, 40.

11. Galatians 4:4 and John 1:14.

Son, made for himself a "true body and a reasonable soul"[12] and brought with him a gospel that "turned the world upside-down."[13] Jew, Greek, and Roman—politician, philosopher, and fisherman—child, teen, and adult—all were confronted by the message proclaimed by Christ.

Jesus and His Disciples

Jesus Christ (c. 4 BC–30 AD) was seen by his followers as the Creator of the universe, the Wisdom and Power of God, the final paschal Lamb, and the risen and everlasting Ruler of all creation. Thus, as his disciples pointed out, his work of atonement for human sin can be effective for and understood by any human anywhere, anytime. Greek philosophers, however, tended to stumble over it in their quest for salvation by wisdom. To them, the teaching of Christ seemed like foolishness.[14] The apostle Paul, born a Hebrew in the Greek city of Tarsus and educated by the famous Gamaliel, attempted to reach the Greeks with the Christian gospel. He saw their insatiable interest in philosophy as an opportunity and proceeded to preach Christ to Stoics, Epicureans, and anyone else who gathered daily in the marketplace in Athens.[15] Some rejected Paul's message, but others saw in the Logos of God the logic, the reason, and the wisdom for which they had been searching.

Defining and refining Judeo-Christian doctrine in a world of Greco-Roman dominance generated lively discussion. Paul addressed not only Stoics and Epicureans, but the growing sect of Gnostics as well. Their spirit/body // good/evil dichotomy resulted either in an ascetic or a lascivious lifestyle, either of which would probably shorten one's earthly existence, whereupon the spirit would be free. Paul denounced the false humility and stringent regulations of the ascetics in a letter to the Colossian church, and

12. *Westminster Shorter Catechism, # 22.*

13. Acts 17:6.

14. 1 Corinthians 1:18–25.

15. Acts 17:16ff.

opposed the wild orgies of the libertines when he wrote to the Galatians.[16] He insisted that soul and body, both created by God, are good; in fact, everything God created is good and is not to be rejected.[17] Christian doctrine does not repudiate the material world; if it did, the incarnation of Christ and the resurrection of the glorified human body would be abominations, and the entire system would crumble.

Church Fathers

Questions of the origin, nature, and destination of the human soul perplexed not only Greek and Roman thinkers who looked back to Plato and Aristotle for answers, but also some who dabbled in Christianity and others who truly followed Christian precepts as well.

A mid-second-century author, Marcion, though claiming to follow the teachings of the apostle Paul, held the Platonic doctrine that considered the human soul to be of the very substance of God, but envisioned the Old Testament God as an inferior demiurge (artisan creator). Some of his ideas also corresponded to those of Gnostics, holding that material flesh is evil and eternal spirit is good.

With yet a different perspective, the Manichaeans, followers of the mid-eastern Mani (216–77) of Zoroastrian affinity, conferred both a good and an evil soul on every individual. For them, future events were to bring about the unification of the "elect" with the Light—and the ultimate destruction of the created world.[18]

One of the most interesting of the church fathers, the Alexandrian theologian Origen (c. 185–254), made a more decided attempt to reconcile Greek philosophy with Christianity, for he believed, as did Plato and Philo, in the pre-existence of the human soul, though not an *eternal* pre-existence. In its former state the soul could gain favor with God or incur his displeasure, hence

16. Colossians 2:16–23; Galatians 5:16–21.

17. 1 Timothy 4:4.

18. Birdsall, "Manichaeism," in Douglas et al., eds., *New International Dictionary*, 625.

the justified inequality of earthly circumstances.[19] As to the future, Origen held to the position of universal salvation in a restored creation. Perhaps animals are included therein.[20]

Within unquestioned Christian parameters lie Justin Martyr (100–165) who was converted from Platonism to Christianity, with its biblical understanding of the soul. Shortly thereafter, Tertullian (165–220), an eminent theologian of Carthage, originated the doctrine of "traducianism," which teaches that both soul and body derive from parents by reproduction.[21] He believed that the innate properties of the soul include freedom of the will, immortality, instinct of dominion, and power of divination.[22]

Another possible explanation for the source of the soul is termed "creationism" by which each individual soul is directly created by God and is subject to corruption by its contact with the body. Jerome (345–419), famous translator of the Vulgate Bible, held this view; and it is said that his contemporary and the most perceptive philosopher of the early church, Aurelius Augustine (354–430), bishop of the city of Hippo in North Africa, preferred it to the doctrine of traducianism, but saw it as inconsistent with the doctrine of original sin.[23]

Augustine saw a need to distinguish the concept of "soul" from that of the "image of God." Even though he stated that "beasts and trees [are] void of intelligence, sensation, or life," he affirmed that "the same God who created the universal cosmos created also

---

19. For information on Origen, see Schaff, *History*, Vol. I, 246; Humphry, *Doctrine of a Future State*, 205, 216.

20. For further study on the doctrine of universalism, read MacDonald, *Evangelical Universalist*.

21. Almond, *Heaven and Hell*, 10. Traducianism, pre-existence, and immediate creationism are the three main explanations for the origin of the human soul, and each was maintained by eminent fathers of the church. Problems include the divisibility (or lack thereof) of the souls of parents, the cessation of God's work of creation at the end of the sixth day, free will in the pre-existent soul, and the doctrine of original sin. Speculation on the origin of the soul appears whenever there is interest in its future.

22. Schaff, *History*, Vol. I, 246.

23. Humphry, *Future Life*, 216. Also, Almond, *Heaven and Hell*, 11.

all the animals, souls as well as bodies." But he proceeded to specify that "among the terrestrial animals man was made by Him in His own image. . . . For He created for him a soul *endowed with reason and intelligence,* so that he might excel all the creatures of earth, air, and sea, which were not so gifted."[24] The soul of the animal, then, is not equivalent to the human soul, for Augustine considered the soul that "was endowed with reason and intelligence" (i.e., the human soul) as synonymous with the "image of God." Via the image, human beings could know God and receive forgiveness, salvation, and eternal life, but lacking reason and intelligence, non-humans could not. Augustine's definition of the soul as an immortal moral agent, attributable only to human beings, has remained standard in the church.

Theodore of Mopsuestia (c. 350–428), a controversial contemporary of Augustine, struggled with the tangled relationship of mortality and sin and seemed to accept the contradictions that mortality was the result of sin and that sin was the result of mortality.[25] The statement that "mortality is chronologically prior to sin, but sin is logically prior to mortality" contributes to the idea that death was an integral part of the natural created world and the accepted fate of the non-human creatures, while immortality was an intrinsic feature of human salvation.[26] Again, the conclusion is that animals have no future after their life on earth.

Fact or Fiction?

Perhaps the last famous Christian living during the rule of the Roman Empire was Patrick (386?/390?–461?/471?), the saint who was so instrumental in bringing the gospel to Ireland—not that that was his original intention! He had been captured from his home in Britain by some pirates, taken to Ireland, and kept as a slave tending a pig farm for six years, then managed to escape

24. Augustine, *City of God,* Book 12, chapters 4 and 23 (trans Dods).
25. Pelikan, *The Christian Tradition,* 234–35.
26. Pelikan, *The Christian Tradition,* 235.

to France on a ship full of Irish wolfhounds! Perhaps he saw the animals as his rescuers! Years later, after a vision of Irish people begging him to return to Ireland, and after attending a seminary, he did return to Ireland, established monasteries, and witnessed the conversion of vast numbers of people. We do not know Patrick's view of animal immortality, but interesting legends about his interactions with animals have developed (specifically his promise that a friend's dog would be in heaven), indicating that at least some of his spiritual descendants thought, or even knew, that he loved animals. Perhaps it was they themselves who loved animals, and were relying on Patrick's having taught them the truth about God and His creation. In any case, as the barbarian movement covered all of western Europe, Ireland was the most steadfast in retaining the Christian faith.

Patrick died in 471; the Roman Empire "fell" in 476.

So it was that the conundrums, the reasoning, and the knowledge of Greco-Roman minds filtered through a barbarian lens and paved the way to the additional queries of medieval minds.

5

Medieval Minds

Great is the Lᴏʀᴅ and most worthy of praise. . . . The Lᴏʀᴅ
is faithful to all his promises and loving toward all he has
made. . . . The eyes of all look to you. . . . You open your
hand and satisfy the desires of every living thing . . . .

PSALM 145:3, 13b, 15, 16.

A Thousand Years!

The political history of the eight to ten centuries that we call the
Middle Ages (c. 500–c. 1400) is a fascinating story of efforts to
maintain centralized power, its breakdown, its semi-re-estab-
lishment under Charlemagne, its breakdown again, the rise of
commerce and of towns, and ultimately the rise of nation states,
morphing into a somewhat familiar European map. However, during this millennium, the uniting factor of western Europe was not
the political scene, but the church, with its center in Rome and a
widespread variety of monasteries and monks.

Early Middle Ages

If St. Patrick and his wolfhounds constitute the epilogue for the Roman world, perhaps Isidore, Archbishop of Seville (560–636), can stand as the prologue to the European world of the Middle Ages. A learned and prolific author, St. Isidore stands out as the most illustrious academic of its early years. In his twenty-volume *Etymologiae*, Volume XII is entitled *Of Beasts and Birds*, and Isidore himself is often depicted, pen in hand, surrounded by a swarm of bees! The accepted explanation is not that Isidore loved bees, but that when he was a child, his father visualized him as a beehive, with honey pouring out of his mouth and attracting a swarm of bees, and believed this to be a sign that Isidore would become a great teacher, which in fact he did. In any case, interest in and importance of animals was manifested in various ways during the Middle Ages, especially in the realms of love and responsibility.

In Ireland and Scotland, the Celtic church as the heir of St. Patrick was distinct from Rome until the Synod of Whitby in 664, and had its own famous monasteries at Iona, Whitby, Jarrow, and Lindisfarne. When the North Sea is low, Lindisfarne is connected to the mainland, but at high tide, it becomes a relatively inaccessible island. Nonetheless, its prior, St. Cuthbert (634–87), enjoyed being on an even more remote island, the Inner Farne, "alone with God, the angels, the demons, and the wild creatures." Apparently birds were the focus of his special love, and he cared particularly for endangered eider ducks, who for centuries thereafter were known as St. Cuthbert's ducklings.

The Venerable Bede (672–735), who lived at the monastery of Jarrow for his entire life, also gives insight into the importance of animals in medieval life. In his *History of the English Church and People* he recounts the story of the Christian King Oswald of Northumbria who died in battle protecting his kingdom from the heathen King Penda of Mercia. Thereafter, so Bede tells us, the place where Oswald died was blessed with healing power—exemplified in the story of a man who was riding near that place and whose horse suddenly rolled over in great pain, apparently dying.

In the final throes of death, the horse's body touched the exact spot where Oswald had been killed—and immediately the horse leapt back to life![1] What a blessing for both man and beast!

However, the major issue concerning animals in the Middle Ages did not revolve around miracles or even love and companionship, but rather the essence of the soul, spirit, knowledge, responsibility, moral behavior, and possible immortality.

Untangling Medieval Trials

The topic of moral behavior was of prime consideration throughout the church, since it is understood that a sense of morality depends upon the knowledge of good and evil, right and wrong, and carries with it legal responsibility. The possibility of attributing this to animals in medieval thought and practice has stimulated some intriguing research in subsequent centuries, continuing into our own day.

From descriptions of a destroyed fresco in a French chapel, an etching showing a sow on trial before a village tribunal was made and used as the frontispiece for *L'Homme et la Bête*, an 1872 volume by Arthur Mangin,[2] considering the natures of human and animal. The etching prompted linguist and University of Michigan professor Edward P. Evans to research and publish a book entitled *The Criminal Prosecution and Capital Punishment of Animals* (1906), documenting animal trials in Europe from the ninth century on. He catalogued cases involving bulls, cows, dogs, horses, pigs (the most numerous), locusts, worms, eels, grasshoppers, rats, and mice, and attested to the fact of their condemnation and executions by criminal courts as recently as the latter half of the nineteenth century in eastern Europe. In cases of infestations of weevils, slugs, and other pests, ecclesiastical courts anathematized the creatures rather than exercising the power of excommunication, which was reserved for errant human beings. In a more

---

1. Bede, *History*, 153.
2. Mangin, *L'Homme et la Bête*. Frontispiece.

recent study of the subject, *Les Procès d'animaux du moyen âge à nos jours* (1970), author Jean Vartier has pointed out that underlying the priestly intervention of the church was the assumption that since the creatures belonged to God, it was God's prerogative to exterminate them, which, in numerous instances, he apparently did.[3] Cases of murder and bestiality received the capital sentence.

Professor Evans made the further interesting observation that courts of law (or some legitimate ruling entity), though considering animals irrational, often treated them as though they were responsible for their actions. He cited the Mosaic Law in the Old Testament stipulating that an animal that kills a human being must be stoned, and notes that this law became the precedent in some later societies.[4] He made two points that he thought should be obvious: first, if animals can be adjudged guilty of crime, Evans reasoned that they must have been considered moral beings; and secondly, if they are liable to judicial punishment for injuries against humans, they should also enjoy legal protection from human cruelty.[5] Although Evans acknowledged the biblical command to stone a dangerous bull as precedent for legal action in medieval and early modern society, he overlooked or ignored the biblical commands of protection for animals spelled out in the Pentateuch (see chapter on the Torah).[6]

According to Yale philosopher J. J. Finkelstein, Evans overlooked another matter, namely the reason for which the Bible demands stoning as the punishment even for unintentional killing: it was a public crime against the order of society and had to be punished publicly.[7] But along with Evans, Finkelstein clarifies the two distinct categories of medieval animal trials: first, cases of insects and other agricultural pests that caused crop failure and could be removed only by supernatural intervention, usually prayer and

---

3. Vartier, *Procès d'animaux du moyen âge à nos jours.*

4. Exodus 21:28, and Evans, *Evolutional Ethics*, 12.

5. Evans, *Evolutional Ethics*, 13.

6 Exodus 20:10; 22:4, 14; 23:4, 5,12; 25:4; Deuteronomy 22:1-4, 6, 10; cf. Proverbs 12:10.

7. Num 35:16ff. Finkelstein, *The Ox That Gored*, 26.

pronouncement of anathemas by the church; and secondly, cases involving identifiable individuals, mostly homicidal animals, who could be apprehended and prosecuted without recourse to supernatural means.[8] Overall, Finkelstein demonstrated that the biblical law pertaining to homicidal animals was the basis of European law, not because the animal was considered a moral being but because its crime violated the structure of society. Moral consequences must devolve upon the owner.

Thus the question remained: if an animal bears responsibility for its actions, does that presuppose belief that animals have a knowledge of good and evil, which in turn would presuppose the presence of a soul, which in turn would presuppose immortality? To examine this, we must move from the courts of law to the cloisters of love and the classrooms of logic.

High Middle Ages

Into the generally Augustinian theological system of the Roman Catholic Church and its official Christian doctrine, there appeared in the thirteenth century two individuals whose concepts of the natural world challenged the status quo and have continued to influence opposing arguments ever since. Francis of Assisi (1182–1226), founder of the Franciscan order, is popularly hailed as the patron saint of ecology, yet often considered the most irrational mystic in all of church history. On the other hand, the Dominican Thomas Aquinas (1225–74) is lauded as Christianity's keenest philosopher and theologian, yet sometimes blamed for all the exploitative raping of the earth that has taken place in the past eight hundred years.[9]

8. Finkelstein, *The Ox That Gored*, 65.

9. Singer, *Animal Liberation*, 201–4. Note that although Singer wrote an excellent volume on compassion for animals, and seems to comprehend St. Francis's position, he does not understand Scripture and has greatly misinterpreted Aquinas.

Francis of Assisi

Poverty, humility, and simplicity were the qualities that Francis of Assisi required of himself and of his brethren in an effort to recapture the purity of Christ, who was always at the center of his devotion.[10] In his extreme mysticism, Francis even identified with the person of Christ to the extent of experiencing a type of re-enactment of the crucifixion by means of the stigmata.[11] Emphasizing the compassion of Christ in his relationships with people and animals, he treated all living things with tenderness; and the stories of his preaching to birds and fish, his taming of wild beasts, and his gentle love are legendary.

Francis's written works include his *Rules* (for the Franciscan Order), the *Admonitions*, the *Testaments*, letters to various people, and several poems of praise including the "Canticle of Creation," which remains popular to this day.[12] In the "Canticle," Francis referred to sun, moon, stars, wind, air, water, fire, and earth (which explicitly included fruit, flowers, and herbs) as brothers and sisters, thus emphasizing their unity with human beings in God's creative acts. And elsewhere Francis often spoke of various animals as "brother" and "sister." A problem could be raised by his referral also to death as a sister, since death was not an original part of the Edenic order; but it is conceivable that Francis was reflecting on the Scripture, "Precious in the sight of God is the death of his saints,"[13] by which a person is brought into the presence of Christ in heaven. It remains unclear, however, whether Francis envisioned any actual eternal brotherhood with the creation.

Additional information about St. Francis is contained in the *Fioretti*, or *Little Flowers*, compiled approximately a century after his death, probably by one or more friars of the Spiritual Party of Franciscans.[14] Of the several tales of Francis's care of animals that

10. Francis, *Little Flowers*, Hudleston and Lavery. Introduction.
11. Francis, *Little Flowers*, 123–60.
12. Francis, *The Writings of St. Francis of Assisi.*
13. Psalm 116:15
14. Francis, *Little Flowers*, vi-vii.

are recorded there, perhaps the taming of the wild wolf of Gubbio is the most revealing of Francis's opinion of animal spirituality. The man-eating wolf that had been terrorizing the people of Gubbio responded meekly to Francis's making the sign of the cross, and proceeded to confess, receive forgiveness, and make a pledge of repentance and obedience. The theological implications of this story are profound: the wolf is sinful, Christ died for the wolf's sins, and the wolf is capable of repentance. Yet Francis (or the friar-author) did not place the wolf on the same level as human beings, for in his accusation against the wolf he stated, "not animals only hast thou destroyed, but thou hast even dared to devour men, made after the image of God."[15] Again, there are various definitions of 'soul' and 'image of God,' but a conclusion, which could easily evoke spirited debate, is that moral responsibility in an animal and the essence of a human being, implying immortality, are not synonymous.

"Nature mystic" is a description that fits Francis well, but biographer E. A. Armstrong (1900–1978) has argued that Francis embodied much more than the affinity to nature that is characteristic of one who admires the natural world. He taught that the love and joy resulting from devotion to God and to the creatures of God should augment a person's love and enjoyment both of God and of the creatures themselves.[16] But merely to categorize Francis as a "nature mystic" and patron saint of ecology is an idea opposed by Lawrence S. Cunningham (b. 1935), professor of theology at the University of Notre Dame, because he sees its scope as too restrictive. Having studied Francis's writings, which though not prolific were profound, Cunningham believes that Francis exerted an impact on medieval spirituality, political theory, art, and literature that goes far beyond the range of an admirer of nature. Moreover, according to Cunningham, his continuing influence in these several areas has been underestimated.[17] Cunningham's appraisal of the *Canticle* is that it does not reflect pantheism, as some have assumed, but an exaltation of Christ himself. Francis kept a

15. Francis, *Little Flowers*, 51.

16. Armstrong, *St. Francis: Nature Mystic*, 242.

17. Cunningham, *St. Francis of Assisi*.

clear distinction between the creature and the Creator, teaching that the purpose of nature is to praise and glorify God.[18] However, while Francis's thought differed vastly from any sort of pantheism, it also differed at least partly from theology arising within the Roman Catholic Church itself.

Thomas Aquinas

Thomas Aquinas, the Catholic Church's greatest theologian, was born just two years before Francis's death, and fifty years later he left volumes of detailed theological studies. As a Dominican intellectual, he devoted his life to teaching and writing, producing commentaries on Scripture and on Aristotle, the *Summa contra Gentiles* (a manual of apologetics), and a monumental systematic theology, *Summa Theologiae*. In the *Summa Theologiae*, Thomas adapted Christianity to an Aristotelian epistemology. Since, according to Aristotle and Thomas, knowledge derives from sense perception, it is not possible to know God except through analogy (similarities between God and man) and negation (defining what God is not). Among many attributes, freedom and volition are shared by God and humans but not by other creatures. Thomas's work was not immediately accepted, but eventually (after much debate) Thomism, rather than Franciscanism, became the dominant philosophical system of the Roman Catholic Church. Thus, Thomas's view of nature is the generally accepted one.

"In nature," wrote St. Thomas, "the less perfect serve the more perfect: plants feed on the earth, animals on plants, and men on both plants and animals."[19] He considered animal ferocity to be the natural order of creation, rather than an effect of Adam's sin. "To think wild and aggressive animals were originally peaceable, not only to men but also to other animals, is quite irrational. . . . Hostility between animals is natural . . . ."[20] Nonetheless, he be-

---

18. Cunningham, *St. Francis of Assisi*, 54–55.

19. Aquinas, *Summa Theologiae*, 146.

20. Aquinas, *Summa Theologiae*, 146.

lieved that all animals were submissive to Adam, as domesticated animals have continued to be to their owners and as Adam was to God as long as he retained his innocence. But only mankind was immortal, "because God gave his soul supernatural ability to preserve his body from decay as long as it itself remained submissive to God" and had access to the Tree of Life.[21] Animal soul consisted only in the element of physical life and bodily sensations, which, while requiring a certain level of sub-rational consciousness, are destroyed by death.

The essential distinction between animal and human in Aquinas's theory lay in the attributes of reason and free will. "Horses lack reason by definition," explained Aquinas, "and a horse endowed with reason wouldn't be a horse."[22] It takes reasoning power and ability to choose in order to reach goals in any active sense. Animals achieve goals passively, behaving in "marvelously clever ways . . . because they are following out superlatively designed processes by natural instinct. But they are not themselves reasoning or choosing, as we see from the fact that all members of the same species behave in the same way."[23] In addition to lacking reason and volition, animals lack the ability to love "with charity," which is the basis for human friendship with God and one's fellow humans. Friendship depends on a common life, shared "only metaphorically" with the creatures; and charity is based on "sharing an eternal happiness of which non-reasoning creatures are incapable."[24] Aquinas affirmed that human beings can love animals and should hold them in honor as creatures of God and servants of man, but bodily death terminates their existence.

21. Aquinas, *Summa Theologiae*, 147.
22. Aquinas, *Summa Theologiae*, 246.
23. Aquinas, *Summa Theologiae*, 188–89.
24. Aquinas, *Summa Theologiae*, 354–55.

John Buridan

Shortly after Aquinas, the French philosopher John Buridan (c. 1200s–post-1358) described the foremost intellectual problem of the late Middle Ages as a struggle to merge the Augustinian and Aristotelian concepts of the soul (i.e. moral agency and rationality) into one "which could be an intimate component of the living body as well as a separable entity liable to judgment on the Day of Reckoning."[25] Buridan himself struggled also with the accepted definition of animal as "sensitive animated substance," because, as he pointed out, this could apply to parts of animals, as worms that become two when cut in half. Also if the soul and body are co-extensive, the loss of part of the body would mean the loss of part of the soul, an impossible situation. Buridan finally insisted on adding the word "entire" to the "sensitive animated substance" to finalize a definition. Having been kept alive in the womb of the mother by the life inherent in her soul (i.e., her physical life), an animal fetus receives a soul of its own at birth and retains that soul no matter how the body might change in size, shape, and color. Death occurs in animals when the soul is destroyed and in humans when the soul departs from the body.[26] Buridan thus reaffirmed St. Thomas's conclusions.

Robert Bellarmine

Two hundred years later, a brilliant Jesuit scholar, bishop, and cardinal, Robert Bellarmine (1542–1621), produced numerous works that have remained influential in the Roman Catholic Church: explanations of the decisions of the Council of Trent,[27] commentaries on the Psalms, and several works of a more spiritual and pious character.

The book in which Bellarmine expounded on God's purposes for the natural world is *The Mind's Ascent to God* (1614).

25. Sobol, *Buridan*, xxiii.

26. Sobol, *Buridan*, xli-xlv

27. Donnelly, *Bellarmine*, 14.

With very tender wording, Bellarmine wrote of the variety of individual specimens of plants, grains, flowers, fruit, and animals, and exhorted his readers to "raise the eyes of your mind to God in whom are the patterns of all things and from whom as from a font of infinite richness there flows that nearly infinite variety."[28] "How clever, although tiny, are ants, spiders, bees, and flies," exclaimed this learned scholar with obvious delight. And these little insects not only have legs, a head, and a heart, but "in their own way prudence and judgment."[29] Insects, all other animals, and even *all inanimate creatures serve and obey* God.[30] Furthermore, God implanted in all animals "an intense love of their offspring." But Bellarmine distinguished sharply between this love, which he perceived as "a love of concupiscence," and charity, the queen of virtues, which is exercised only by human beings, and without which, as Aquinas taught, no one can live eternally.[31] Since animals "know nothing at all about the love of friendship," God's purpose in giving them love for their offspring was to preserve the species "like a shadow of eternity."[32] The shadow of eternity was all that Bellarmine allowed to animals, for "the souls of brute animals perish with the body," and apart from God and the angels, human beings are the only creatures in the universe who are granted immortality. "Great is the dignity of the soul," observed Bellarmine, "since by it man is like God and unlike the beasts."[33] This orthodox theologian did not despise even despicable creatures, however, and it has been recorded that he patiently permitted fleas to bite him, explaining, "We shall have heaven to reward us for our sufferings, but these poor creatures have nothing but the enjoyment of the present life."[34]

28. Donnelly, *Bellarmine*, 70.

29. Donnelly, *Bellarmine*, 187.

30. Donnelly, *Bellarmine*, 136.

31. Donnelly, *Bellarmine*, 248.

32. Donnelly, *Bellarmine*, 191.

33. Donnelly, *Bellarmine*, 133.

34. Tylor, *Primitive Culture*, Vol. I, 471.

Conclusion

The piety and power of the church throughout the Middle Ages (and with Bellarmine as a later example) produced a unity that pervades many pages of western history. However, certain unfortunate developments ultimately occurred that shifted actual guidance of thought and action from ecclesiastical authority to individualized expression. The Great Schism of the church, the struggle within the papacy, and monetary corruption combined with the rise of commerce and aspirations of authority, especially in Italy, led to momentous changes in European society. When Dante, the famous author of the *Divine Comedy*, placed Pope Boniface in the eighth level of hell in his *Inferno*, it was nothing less than a brazen slam at the church, and when the church itself ordered the execution of one of its own faithful, Girolamo Savonarola, the stage was set for the movements known as the Renaissance and the Reformation.

---- **6** ----

Reformational Re-examination

The grass withers and the flowers fall,
but the word of our God stands forever.

—ISAIAH 40:8

A Renewed Unity

Renaissance literature and art are fascinating. Concurrent strug-
gles of the Roman Catholic Church are distressing. Then unfold-
ing throughout the sixteenth century, the Protestant Reformation
challenged both Renaissance humanism and Roman Catholic
theology. As heir to the individualism of the Renaissance as well as
herald of a new unity centered on the Judeo-Christian Scriptures,
the reformers posited the Bible as the sole and ultimate authority
of truth that unified believers, while its very teaching on the priest-
hood of all believers opened the door to diversity. While granting
individual freedom, it is *Scripture* that unifies Protestant believers,
not church tradition, nor any particular view of politics, sacra-
ments—or Nature.

Within the Protestant context for the ensuing centuries there appeared from time-to-time spokesmen for the plight of animals and apologists for their creational equality with humankind and their ultimate destiny. Basic tenets of Protestantism led certain church leaders to defend the concept of the animal soul, or at least to affirm an afterlife of happiness for them. Their teaching on this subject was not widely known, however, for other doctrinal issues and other developments in European society overshadowed the animal question. But because those who found warrant for a blissful hereafter for the "brute beasts" were among the most famous and influential of the Protestant theologians, their writings are crucial in support of the idea, and we will focus specifically on Martin Luther (1483–1546), Martin Bucer (1491–1551), John Bradford (1510–55), and John Calvin (1509–64).

Martin Luther

In his popular *Table Talk*, Martin Luther commented on the purposes for which God created various things. Fruits and herbs supplied food for man and beast; animals were made in order to inspire mankind to praise God; stars themselves praise God; and "whereunto serve the ravens and crows, but to call upon the Lord who nourishes them."[1] Luther confirmed with 1 Timothy 4:4 that "every creature of God is good" and becomes "vain, evil, noxious, etc., without its fault and from the outside" only because "man does not judge and evaluate it rightly and because he enjoys it in a wrong way."[2] "For created things are good in themselves," emphasized Luther, "and those who know God know also the things of nature not as something vain, but as they are in truth; and they use them but do not take advantage of them."[3]

Unlike Thomas Aquinas, Luther believed that the source of pain, misery, and the ferocity of animals does not lie in the natural

1. Luther, *Table Talk*, 58.

2. Luther, *Romans*, 238.

3. Luther, *Romans*, 238.

order of things, but in the sin of humanity itself. It was human sin that corrupted the peaceful creation. Animals, even in their killing of each other, are innocent; humans are guilty. Then in his *Lectures on Romans*, Luther identified the word "creature" as the entire created universe, and predicated the word "vanity" only to mankind. In the *Commentary on Genesis*, he taught that the *image* of God in man, and *its* resultant immortality, was ruined by Adam's fall into sin, but it could begin to be restored in the present life by the power of the Gospel and perfected in heaven. And because only humans were created in God's *image*, immortality is a gift only to humans. Once again, we see the difficulty of grasping the idea of "image" as compared to "soul," but again, that comparison is a separate issue to be studied. Luther simply observed in his discussion of the creation of Eve that it is "clear that she has a share in immortality, a life better than that of the remaining animals, which live only their animal life, without hope of eternal life."[4]

On the other hand, Luther also observed that with human perfection (i.e., in heaven) "it will come to pass also that all creatures shall be more subject unto us, than ever they were unto Adam in paradise."[5] Is it conceivable then, in spite of such contradictory statements, that Luther reserved the possibility of animal participation in eternity? Luther certainly held to the inerrancy of Scripture, undoubtedly affirming the truth of Isaiah 11:1–10, Romans 8:21, and numerous other passages that apply to the future life of non-human creatures.

Martin Bucer and John Bradford

Enthusiastically adopting Lutheran reform was the Dominican monk Martin Bucer. When excommunicated from the Roman Catholic Church, he sought refuge at the free city of Strasbourg, and soon became a leader in the Protestant movement. His influence spread throughout Europe as he became known for his

4. Luther, *Luther's Works*, Vol. I, 117. See also 56–57
5. Kerr, *A Compend of Luther's Theology*, 83.

peace-making efforts and his effect on theological developments, particularly in England and in Switzerland. Exiled in 1548, Bucer went to England at Archbishop Thomas Cranmer's (1489–1556) request, was appointed Regius professor of divinity at Cambridge, and worked closely with Anglican academics during the reign of Edward VI.[6] There, for two years, Bucer had direct influence on the English reformer John Bradford.

John Bradford (1519–55), fellow of Pembroke Hall, soon became known for his staunch reformed views, earnest preaching, and gentle character, and was licensed to preach, serving as royal chaplain from 1551 until his arrest in 1553. Condemned to the stake by Queen Mary I in 1555, Bradford spent his last days writing the "Restoration of All Things," much of which was a translation of parts of Bucer's *Commentary on Romans* (1536).[7] In his exposition of Romans 8:19–22, the passage in which the apostle Paul states that the entire creation will be "brought into the glorious freedom of the children of God" (i.e. eternal life), Bradford explained that his "cogitation in this matter [is] not mine only, but the cogitation of one who was my father in the Lord," giving in a footnote a lengthy quotation in Latin from Bucer's *Metaphysics*.

For Scriptural support of the presence of animals in the eternal state, Bradford referenced Isaiah 65:17ff, Ephesians 1:10, Acts 3:21, and 2 Peter 3:13. Commenting on the passage in 2 Peter, he emphasized that the world would be renewed and took this to mean that the restoration of all things is "so manifest, that no man can well deny it."[8] Specifying "plants, animals, and other things having life" in the resurrection, which "doubtless shall be adorned by the whole shape of the world 'delivered from corruption,'"[9] Bradford contentedly reflected that "it is enough and enough for me, that I,

---

6. For Bucer's influence on the English Reformation, see the introduction to the translation of the *Common Places of Martin Bucer*, edited by David F. Wright.

7. Bucer, *Common Places*, 466.

8. Bradford, *Writings,*356.

9. Bradford, *Writings*, 355. This is also noted as wording taken from the *Catechismus Brevis* of 1553.

and all the whole world with me, shall be much more happy than now I can by any means conceive."

It was John Bradford, building on Bucer's theology, who offered detailed answers to several of Aquinas's objections. Aquinas believed that the heavenly bodies and the elements would be restored because they were created incorruptible (i.e., eternal). Mankind will also be renewed because his soul is incorruptible, "but beasts, plants, &c. are corruptible (i.e. temporal) both wholly and in every part: therefore they were not made to incorruption; . . . and so are they not conformable to the renewing, . . . and therefore they shall not be restored."[10] Bradford asked how Thomas would be able to prove his conjecture, and observed that "the nature and being of all things dependeth on the omnipotency of God . . . [who] made all things of nothing: and therefore heaven and the celestial bodies have no more of themselves that they be perpetual, than have those things that last but a day,"[11] and "cannot he . . . give hereafter to the things that he hath made that whereof now in themselves they have no capacity?"[12]

Bradford also addressed Aquinas's objection that "if beasts and plants shall be restored, either all or some shall be restored. If all shall be restored, then must . . . the same in number be restored; which is not convenient."[13] (Note that the use of the word "convenient" comes from the Latin which means "fitting, suitable, agreed upon.") And further that if only some are restored, and there is no reason why some would be and others would not, Aquinas decided "therefore, they shall not be restored." Bradford asked the obvious: how does Aquinas know it is not "convenient" for God to restore all, "in that this thing wholly resteth in the hand and will of God."[14] In a third objection, Thomas had appealed to Aristotle who maintained that "the perpetuity of things . . . hangs on the continual moving of heaven," which, because "the moving of heaven shall

10. Bradford, *Writings*, 358, note 2.
11. Bradford, *Writings*, 359.
12. Bradford, *Writings*, 360. Note that Butler echoes this argument.
13. Bradford, *Writings*, 360.
14. Bradford, *Writings*, 361.

cease," Aquinas concluded, "in these inferior things no perpetuity may be looked for." Bradford counted this as mere conjecture since it cannot be proven by the Word of God. Finally, the great Dominican asserted that "beasts and plants were made for the sustentation of the mutual life of man: but this life shall cease, therefore shall they also."[15] In return, Bradford queried, "Who knoweth whether God have made them to none other 'end' or use?" Bradford could have satisfied his own query and strengthened his argument by reminding his readers that Scripture itself asserts that the heavens declare the glory of God, that nature actually reveals God's "invisible qualities," and that God created all things for his own pleasure.[16] Instead, this young scholar, soon to die at the stake, chose to share with his readers a prayer of confidence that the Holy Spirit would lead us "into this and all other necessary truth."[17]

John Calvin

John Calvin (1509–64), the undisputed systematician of reformed theology, also delved into the nature and purpose of the universe. He spent three very formative years of his life in Strasbourg, learning from Bucer, before returning to Geneva for his most productive years of teaching. His views pertaining to the natural world appear in the *Tracts and Treatises* (1534ff), in his preface to Olivetan's translation of the New Testament (1535), and in the *Institutes* (begun in 1536 and expanded throughout his life). Book I of the *Institutes* is entitled "The Knowledge of God the Creator," which knowledge Calvin recognized as the only access to happiness and the final goal of the blessed life.[18] God displayed knowledge of himself by his creative acts, so that "wherever you cast your eyes, there is no spot in the universe wherein you cannot discern at

15. Bradford, *Writings*, 362.

16. Psalm 19:1; Romans 1:20; Revelation 4:11.

17. Bradford, *Writings*, 364.

18. Calvin, *Institutes I*, 51.

least some sparks of his glory."[19] He referred to Psalm 19, which attributes knowledge to the sky itself, and to Romans 1:19–20 where the apostle Paul affirmed that "what men need to know concerning God has been disclosed to them" through the creation of the world.[20] Citing the academic disciplines of astronomy, medicine, and all natural science as means of viewing God's glory, he maintained that even "common folk and the most untutored . . . cannot be unaware of the excellence of divine art."[21] Thus the primary purpose of Nature is to display the glory of God.

The natural world would show God's glory whether human beings were present or not. But because there are human beings, Nature has an additional purpose, that of providing for human needs, the first of which is knowledge of God himself. So, when God "disposed the movements of the sun and stars to human uses, filled the earth, waters, and air with living things, and brought forth an abundance of fruits to suffice as foods," God showed his fatherly goodness to mankind.[22] Calvin pointed out that "before he fashioned man" God prepared everything that would be "useful and salutary for him."[23] And since Calvin had established at the very outset of the *Institutes* that the basic human need is knowledge of God, he affirmed therefore that man's first use of Nature is contemplation. Calvin exhorted all his readers "first of all [to] follow the universal rule, not to pass over in ungrateful thoughtlessness or forgetfulness those conspicuous powers which God shows forth in his creatures, and then learn so to apply it to themselves that their very hearts are touched."[24] The creatures are like mirrors of God's wisdom, justice, goodness, and power which we should ponder "at length, . . . seriously, . . . faithfully, . . . repeatedly."[25] That human beings are to contemplate Nature and God's attributes

19. Calvin, *Institutes I,* 52.

20. Calvin, *Institutes I,* 53 and Romans 1:19–20.

21. Calvin, *Institutes I,* 53.

22. Calvin, *Institutes I,* 162.

23. Calvin, *Institutes I,* 182.

24. Calvin, *Institutes I,* 181.

25. Calvin, *Institutes I,* 180.

reflected therein while not falling into the sin of worshipping the created things themselves, Calvin made abundantly clear in his opposition to pagan philosophy and practices.[26]

None of Calvin's works purport to be a theology of Nature, per se; the more immediately necessary doctrines of Scripture and soteriology occupied his time. In explaining the nature of the human soul, however, he made frequent contrast to the soul of animals. He defined the human soul as an "immortal yet created essence" which is aware of God, discerns good from evil, and "grasps things that are right, just, and honorable."[27] The soul is the seat of intelligence and rationality, which Calvin decided was the difference between man and animal.[28] Even though man's nature has been corrupted by sin, yet there is "implanted in human nature some sort of desire to search out the truth," and "human understanding possesses some power of perception" which is totally lacking in animals.[29] The conclusion was that "reason is proper to [human] nature" and "distinguishes us from brute beasts, just as they by possessing feeling differ from inanimate things."[30]

The subject of immortality Calvin covered thoroughly in his treatise on "Psychopannychia," or "soul sleep," the belief that at the death of the body, the soul slips into an unconscious sleep, body and soul both remaining in the grave until the final resurrection that will take place at the return of Jesus Christ. This doctrine became popular during the Reformation era among some branches of Protestantism, but Calvin in his essay surveyed the pertinent Scripture and refuted the idea masterfully.[31] Part of the refutation lies in an explanation of immortality, which he attributed to

26. Calvin, *Institutes I*, 5; 3; 24.

27. Calvin, *Institutes I*, 185.

28. Calvin, *Institutes II*, 270.

29. Calvin, *Institutes II*, 271.

30. Calvin, *Institutes II*, 276.

31. Almond explains the Calvinist (and Anglican) position well but gives only Luke 23:43 (Jesus' promise to the thief on the cross) and Luke 16:22 (the story of the beggar Lazarus) as Scriptural support. Other weighty references to immediate presence with the Lord are Philippians 1:23 and 2 Corinthians 5:4–8.

humans but not to animals.[32] Because the soul of man possesses reason, intellect, and will (non-physical properties) it continues to live after the death of the physical body, *in an intermediate state*, to be rejoined with the body at the resurrection. But because the animal soul does not possess those human properties, it does not live *during the intermediate state*. Thus Calvin maintained that only human beings are actually *immortal*, that is, remaining conscious throughout *both the intermediate and eternal states*.

What then of animals? If they are not conscious during the intermediate state, does this mean that they have no future life? Calvin certainly recognized the implications of Romans 8:19–21 that "everything in heaven and on earth strives after renewal"[33] and that although Calvin denied that creatures are "endowed with any perception,"[34] he wrote elsewhere that the "animals, and even inanimate creatures—even trees and stones—conscious of the emptiness of their present existence, long for the final day of resurrection, to be released from emptiness with the children of God."[35] And further, "because the creatures are subject to corruption . . . and also because they have a hope of being freed hereafter from corruption, it follows that they groan . . . until they have been delivered."[36] Deliverance and being freed hereafter are hardly descriptive of annihilation.

What Calvin actually succeeded in doing was to pinpoint the distinction between the immortality of the human soul and the glorified restoration of all created things at the end of time, the "new heaven and new earth" as specified by the apostle Peter. Calvin, by his definition of the human soul, denied *immortality* to non-human creatures; but by his phrases, "they have a hope of being freed hereafter" and "until they have been delivered," he accepted the concept of the presence of animals in *eternity*. Undoubtedly God has the power to restore animals whose bodies died long

32. Calvin, *Tracts and Treatises*, 3, 450–51.

33. Calvin, *Institutes III*, xxv, 2, 989.

34. Calvin, *Institutes III*, 989.

35. Calvin, *Institutes III*, 717.

36. Wilson, *Romans*, 144.

ago even if they have no consciousness during the *intermediate* state. Remember also that the word "hope" as used in Romans 8:21 means not a vague wish, but undeniable assurance.[37]

A Concluding Surprise

In grappling with many theological issues, the Reformers did not overlook the necessity of understanding the purposes and predicaments of the natural world, its importance and ultimate destiny, as well as the present problem of suffering in this lifetime. Common Christian teaching on suffering in the animal world is that it came as part of the curse of God subsequent to human sin. Yet to pass such a knotty problem off so perfunctorily seemed too superficial to the Genevan reformer, and he made an additional observation, inserted in a most intriguing comment. Calvin's brief but clear statement that animals "are bearing part of the punishment deserved by man" is worthy of reflection. He linked this suffering to the idea that animals were created for man's use, especially in the sacrificial system of the Old Testament—and it cannot escape one's notice that the "punishment deserved by man" is not in fact borne by man, but by Christ. The statement therefore positions animals in a *parallel* form of the innocence, mediatorial work, and eternal life of Jesus Christ. The mystery of the sacrificial Lamb is not without deep significance in the truly *longue durée* of the mind of God.

37. See the final paragraph of the preface.

— 7 —

Anglican Additions

Praise the Lord from the earth, you great sea creatures,
. . . wild animals and all cattle,
small creatures and flying birds. . . .
Let them praise the name of the Lord,
for his name alone is exalted.

—PSALM 148:7–12

A Widening World

THE HISTORY OF EUROPE in the sixteenth to eighteenth centuries is intensely interesting, seething with political intrigue, intermarriage of royal families, religious controversies, and eager explorations and claims in the New World. As far as Christian organizations were concerned, the Roman Catholic Church held on to Italy, Spain, and France (in spite of Gallican confrontation), Holland went to the Calvinists, Germany was divided between Roman Catholics and Lutherans, and England was declared Anglican by King Henry VIII. Through it all, theological discussion proceeded. And within the Anglican fold, bishops, philosophers, poets, and colonists all weighed in on the question of the position of animals in God's wider kingdom.

Joseph Butler

According to biographer Terence Penulhum, Bishop Joseph Butler (1692–1752) was Anglicanism's greatest philosopher and theologian. Perhaps best known for his *Analogy of Religion* (1736) and essays on "Personal Identity" and "Virtue," Butler directed much of his writing against impersonal and materialistic explanations of life. Butler's burden was to show that the essence of the life, identity, and immortality of human beings does not consist in sense organs or physical capacities. He considered the organs of sense to be "merely instruments" of perception and stated that there is no probability that "the alienation or dissolution of these instruments is the destruction of the [actual] perceiving and moving agent."[1]

However, he recognized that by defining life and identity non-materialistically he had to include animals along with human beings. He pointed out that "things, plants, animals, and people preserve their identities throughout physical life, though they undergo radical changes in size, shape, and capacity."[2] Such changes obviously do not eradicate life or identity. A rhetorical question reveals Butler's subsequent train of thought: "Why should death be any different?" Life and identity do not consist of physical properties.

But, query the objectors, are animals immortal? Butler responded that these objectors think it is "an insuperable difficulty, that they [animals] should be immortal, and by consequence capable of everlasting happiness."[3] But to believe animals incapable of everlasting happiness is "invidious and weak," and Butler proceeded to give reason for their immortality on both natural and moral grounds. Now whether he conceived of the natural world as having been created immediately by God or developed through

---

1. Butler, *Analogy*, 14.

2. Penelhum, *Butler*, 114.

3. Butler, *Analogy*, 15.

some long process is not clear at this point, but he asserted that "we can trace up our own existence to the same original with theirs."[4]

Further, since the attribute of immortality does not necessitate a rational or moral nature, according to Bishop Butler, it makes no difference whether animals are endued with any such qualities, but they may in fact be so endued. There is no way to know. Still, it is noteworthy that this kind of consideration antedates by over a hundred years the studies in animal intelligence and psychology that became popular in the latter nineteenth century.

Christopher Smart

Cambridge-educated but not ordained, Christopher Smart (1722–71) was an Anglican poet who added in verse form some curious contemplations on the topic of animals' relationship to God. Journalist, recipient of the Seaton award for religious poetry on several occasions, and highly competent in Hebrew, Smart was for several years instructor in philosophy, logic, classical literature, and Greek New Testament.[5] He translated the Psalms and wrote hymns for the Church of England that often reflected his love of animals, as for example, his Hymn III for Epiphany:

> Come, ye creatures of thanksgiving,
> Which are harmoniz'd to bless,
> Birds that warble for your living,
> Beasts with ways of love express.
>
> . . .
>
> Brousing kids, and lambkins grazing,
> Colts and younglings of the drove,
> Come with all your modes of praising,
> Bounding through the leafless grove.

Smart's personal faith was highly emotional, his poetry visionary.[6] And while his imaginations sometimes are hardly standard Anglican theology, he does reflect deep knowledge and

4. Butler, *Analogy*, 15.

5. Smart, *Poetical Works*, Williamson, editor, xvi.

6. Douglas et al., eds., *Dictionary of the Christian Church*, 909.

sincere worship. Unfortunately, his profligate lifestyle led him into irremediable debt, and a mental breakdown resulted in confinement in an asylum for the latter years of his life. While in the asylum he wrote voluminously, much of it religious poetry, including the lengthy and charming *Jubilate Agno*, which includes observations on his cat.

> For I will consider my Cat Jeoffry.
> For he is the servant of the Living God duly and daily serving him.
> For at the first glance of the glory of God in the East he worships in his way.
> For this is done by wreathing his body seven times round with elegant quickness.
> For then he leaps up to catch the musk, which is the blessing of God upon his prayer . . . .
> For he purrs in thankfulness, when God tells him he's a good Cat . . . .
> For he knows that God is his Saviour . . . .
> For he is of the Lord's poor and so indeed is he called by benevolence perpetually—Poor Jeoffry! poor Jeoffry! the rat has bit thy throat.
> For I bless the name of the Lord Jesus that Jeoffry is better.
> For the divine spirit comes about his body to sustain it in compleat cat.[7]

Smart even saw the divine spirit in flowers, which play a major role throughout the *Jubilate Agno*. Thus some observations:

> Let Kelita rejoice with Xiphion the Bulbous Iris.
> *For at his second coming his horn will be exalted in* glory.
> Let Bunni rejoice with Bulbine—leaves like leek, purple flower.
> *For Man and Earth suffer together.*[8]

> *For Eternity is like a grain of mustard as a growing body and improving spirit . . . .*
> *For mustard is the proper food of birds and men are bound to cultivate it for their use.*[9]

7. Smart, *Jubilate*, Fragment B, Lines 695–742.

8. Smart, *Jubilate*, Fragment C, Lines 149 and 155.

9. Smart, *Jubilate*, Fragment B, Lines 372 and 618.

And finally, of all things animate and inanimate:

> For all the creatures mentioned by Pliny are somewhere or other extant to the glory of God.
> For the TRUMPET of God is a blessed intelligence and so are all the instruments in HEAVEN.[10]

Richard Dean

With undoubtedly less literary finesse than Smart, but more theological substance, another Anglican approached the topic. This was the curate of Middleton, Richard Dean (1727–78), who in 1767 published "An Essay on the Future Life of Brutes." He substantiated his belief in detail on the weight of three authorities: Scripture, the "ancients," and reason.

Dean began his argument with Romans 8. "The Scriptures plainly intimate that Brute Animals will have a Being in the future, and partake in some Degree of those Benefits which shall be conferred after the universal Change."[11] Commenting on verse 19, Dean believed that "the chief Object of the Creatures' earnest Expectation before-mentioned is, namely, that it is a Freedom or Exemption from the Evils of Instability, Decay, and Dissolution, to which the bodies of living Beings, and all material Forms, are universally subject."[12] Of verse 21, Dean emphasizes that the eventual condition of the animals is *not* decay or dissolution, but enjoyment of the "glorious freedom of the children of God."

Some pages later, Dean answered common objections from Psalm 49 and Ecclesiastes 3. On the question posed in Ecclesiastes 3:21—"Who knows if the spirit of man rises upward and if the spirit of the animal goes down into the earth?"—Dean simply commented, "For ought then that this Question thus put implies to the contrary, the Souls of Brutes may be immortal, as well as the Souls of Men." But Dean chose to emphasize 3:14, "I know

10. Smart, *Jubilate*, Fragment B, Lines 620 and 245.

11. Dean, *Essay*, 3.

12. Dean, *Essay*, 11.

that everything God does will endure forever," by saying, "This is expressly asserting the Eternity of all God's Works."[13] As for Psalm 49, Dean correctly pointed out that the word translated "perish" does not mean annihilation, but "to be forgotten," and has nothing to do with individual life after death.[14]

The argument that animals have no future life because they were created only for the present purposes of mankind, Dean considered a "weak and unwarrantable Conceit." It is true that they do serve man, but "may not God be supposed to have raised this mighty Frame of Things with a Design to diffuse his Goodness, and display his Glory?"[15] Dean rested his case on Revelation 4:11: "thou hast created all things, and for thy pleasure they are and were created."

For objectors who believe that animals cannot be immortal because they are "incapable of religion," Dean wryly, perhaps even humorously, observed that they are no worse off than people who go to church out of habit but have no idea of what has transpired in the service. "For Thousands of those go to Church, only because their Acquaintance go, follow Fathers or Mothers, Uncles or Aunts, as a Dog follows his Master, are as unmindful as this Animal, of what is said or done there, and return Home as ignorant and uninformed as the verriest Brute upon Earth."[16]

Turning to the "ancients," Dean cited four notable voices. First, Philo (c. 20 BC–c. AD 45): "Hereafter, Brute Animals will be divested of their Ferocity, and become tame and gentle, . . . the whole Race of Scorpions, Serpents, and other at present noxious Reptiles, shall become harmless, and have no Power to afflict People with their Stings."[17] Next, Tertullian (c. 160–c. 215): "When the Innocence and Purity of Nature being restored, Beasts shall live in Harmony with Beasts." Then, Origen (c. 185–c. 254): "These great Bodies [sun and moon] also wait for the Manifestation of the Sons

13. Dean, *Essay,* 89–90.
14. Dean, *Essay,* 90.
15. Dean, *Essay,* 69.
16. Dean, *Essay,* 73.
17. Dean, *Essay,* 46–48.

of God." And fourthly, the Jewish Rabbi Manasseh (1604–57): "Dumb Animals will have a much happier State than ever they enjoyed, when Men shall rise again."

Lastly, Dean turned to reason, and argued in opposition to Descartes and Malebranche (see chapter 8), that animals certainly show their thoughts by their behavior, their expressions of pain, and their fear of older animals. Joining Scripture to reason, he affirmed the intelligence of animals by quoting Jeremiah 8:7: "Even the stork in the sky knows her appointed seasons, and the dove, the swift and the thrush observe the time of their migrations. But my people do not know the requirements of the LORD."[18]

Dean ended his *Essay* with three considerations worth pondering. First, if animals are denied immortality because they are inferior to humans, "Man is therefore not intitled to any, because he is inferior to Cherubim."[19] Secondly, when humans look down on a worm, a fly, or a mite, "thou can'st entertain a mean Opinion of no Creature without some Reproach to that Wisdom which contrived it. Remember that it was not a Thing beneath the Dignity of Heaven to create the most diminutive Animal; and how then can it be unbecoming the same adorable Power to continue its Existence? Thy Sentiments, O Man, in this Instance, are the suggestions of Pride, Envy, and Prejudice."[20] In closing, Dean posed the question that if we enjoy Nature now, as it is, "what will it be then, when all the Secrets of Nature are unfolded, when every Thing which God has made is exhibited in its utmost Perfection; and all the Wonders of his wisdom fall within the Compass of human knowledge? . . . If any Thing is certain, it is that the Perfections of God will never be less visible in his Works than they are at present."[21]

18. Dean, *Essay*, 51–61.
19. Dean, *Essay*, 95.
20. Dean, *Essay*, 98.
21. Dean, *Essay*, 84 and 117.

Puritans and Jonathan Edwards

Carrying Reformational theology most clearly into the seventeenth and eighteenth centuries were the English and American Puritans, and because "carving a home out of the wilderness" has been a perennial theme in American life, it is important to consider the Puritans' views of the natural world.

In 1641 the Massachusetts Bay Colony codified its statutes in a "Body of Liberties," which included the protection of animals. Item #92 stipulated that "no man shall exercise any Tirranny or Crueltie towards any bruite Creature which are usuallie kept for man's use," and item #93 specified that all who "leade or drive Cattel" must stop to permit them to rest and be refreshed.[22] As author Roderick Nash points out, only domestic animals, those with utilitarian purpose, were protected, but it is nonetheless significant that this official recognition of the needs and comforts of animals was given at the same time that Descartes' theory of the animal-machine was gaining adherents. Nash suggests that "the task of creating a new society in a wilderness made the Puritans more mindful of comprehensive ethical principles derived from a state of nature similar to the one they occupied."[23] Undoubtedly they were obeying the "comprehensive ethical principles" of Scripture to which in those early years they were fully committed.

However, within a century the descendants of the first Puritans had become enamored of things other than Scripture, and it fell to the scholar-evangelist Jonathan Edwards (1703–58) to call them back to God's Word and to their responsibilities to the Lord. According to historian Perry Miller (1905–63), Edwards was "the greatest philosopher-theologian yet to grace the American scene."[24] Graduate of Yale and proponent of Augustinian Calvinism, he served in three successive pastorates, during which the revivals known as the Great Awakening occurred. His writings,

22. Nash, *Rights of Nature*, 18.

23. Nash, *Rights of Nature*, 18.

24. Quoted by Paul Helm in Douglas et al., eds., *New International Dictionary*, 334.

particularly the *Freedom of the Will*, *Original Sin*, and *Religious Affections*, continue to influence philosophical and religious thought.

From childhood, Edwards had loved the outdoors and although he later disparaged the value of some of the "pious affections" of his youth, it is noteworthy that Jonathan and two other boys "joined together and built a booth in a swamp, in a very retired spot, for a place of prayer."[25] As an older teenager, he found that "often walking alone in the woods" or "in a solitary place in my father's pasture" brought him closer to God. "I often used to sit and view the moon for a long time; and in the day, spent much time in viewing the clouds and sky, to behold the sweet glory of God in these things. . . . And scarce any thing, among all the works of nature, was so sweet to me as thunder and lightning, . . . leading me to sweet contemplations of my great and glorious God."[26] At age twenty, he wrote a series of seventy resolutions which pertain to his relationship to God, many of which center on his interaction with other people, but interestingly number 15 reads: "*Resolved*, Never to suffer the least motions of anger towards irrational beings."[27] In Edwards' contemplations of the Christian life, angry behavior toward creatures is sin, and their lack of reason is no excuse for maltreatment.

In his *Dissertation Concerning the End for Which God Created the World*, Edwards addressed the purpose of Nature: the glory of God. To build his argument, Edwards used the familiar passages in Psalms 104:31 and 148:13, "May the glory of the LORD endure forever; may the LORD rejoice in his works" and "Let them [sun, moon, stars, lightning, winds, trees, animals, cattle, kings, children, etc.] praise the name of the LORD, for his name alone is exalted." He also drew from a long section on creation and providence in Isaiah, where God says, "For my own sake, for my own sake, I do this. . . . I will not yield my glory to another."[28] Paul's doxology in Romans 11 states, "For from him and through him

25. Edwards, *Works*, xii.

26. Edwards, *Works*, xiii.

27. Edwards, *Works*, xxi.

28. Isaiah 48:11.

and to him are all things. To him be the glory forever! Amen."[29] Thus Edwards concludes, "God's glory therefore must be a desirable, valuable consequence of the work of creation. . . . It is manifest . . . that the glory of God is an ultimate end [i.e. purpose] in the creation of the world."[30] And finally he wrote, "Thus we see that the great end of God's works, which is so variously expressed in Scripture, is indeed but ONE; and this *one* end is most properly and comprehensively called, THE GLORY OF GOD."[31]

Edwards approached the present subjection and future liberation of Nature as stated in Romans 8 in *An Humble Attempt to Promote Explicit Agreement and Visible Union of God's People, in Extraordinary Prayer, for the Revival of Religion and the Advancement of Christ's Kingdom on Earth.* He pointed out that the visible world has been "subject to sin and made, as it were, a servant to it, through the abuse that man, who has the dominion over the creatures, puts the creatures to." In his estimation, man abuses sunlight, rain, plants, and animals; thus the world "groans." God has chosen to subject creatures to man's wickedness in order to permit the "stated laws" of Nature to continue for a while, but Edwards lamented that "the creature is abused in it, perverted to far meaner purposes, than those for which the author . . . made and adapted it." Edwards agreed with the apostle Paul in saying that the creature is unwillingly subjected to man's sinful will and "hopes for an alteration."[32] He expressed delight that at the end of time, when Christ's kingship will be evident to all and the children of God receive the promised glorious liberty, "the whole inanimate creation shall greatly rejoice."[33]

29. Romans 11:36.

30. Edwards, *Works*, Vol. I, 112.

31. Edwards, *Works*, Vol. I, 119.

32. Edwards, *Works*, Vol. II, 289.

33. Edwards, *Works*, Vol. II, 290. For further consideration of the "groaning" of the creation, read, contemplate, and enjoy Southgate's book by that title!

John Wesley

Methodism, the popular eighteenth-century movement within and beyond the Church of England, was founded by John Wesley (1703–91). Profoundly influenced by the Calvinist George Whitefield (1714–70) and the Moravian Count Nikolaus von Zinzendorf (1700–1760), Wesley considered the whole world as his parish, and during his fifty-year-long preaching career, it is estimated that he delivered about forty thousand sermons! His open-air preaching reached huge audiences, frequently of previously unchurched people, and his sermons, recorded for posterity, continue to reach countless readers.

Among the topics that Wesley addressed was "The General Deliverance," based on Romans 8:19–22. He began the sermon with the reminder that the Lord's mercy is "over all his works," but that in view of universal misery, this is a perplexing promise. He then divided the sermon into three questions:

I.   What was the original state of the brute creation?

II.   In what state is it at present?

III.   In what state will it be at the manifestation of the children of God?[34]

Wesley's answers are as follows:

First, the original condition of the animals was "paradisaical; perfectly happy." They had understanding, will, liberty, passions, affections. They enjoyed plentiful food and everything that gave them pleasure. And "they too were immortal: For 'God made not death; neither hath he pleasure in the death of any living.'"

Secondly, their present condition is sadly changed. God had appointed mankind as the channel of blessing to the rest of the creation, but when he sinned, the channel was cut, and "those blessings could no longer flow in upon them." Thus, because of human sin, animals' intelligence was diminished, they became irrational and cruel, their outward appearance in many instances grew ugly, and they fled from their common enemy and predator, humanity.

---

34. Wesley, "The General Deliverance," *Works*, 242.

Thirdly, continued Wesley, God forbid that we should affirm or even entertain a thought that the brute creation will remain in this deplorable condition! "Let the plain word of God take place," the preacher urged, "for they shall be delivered from the bondage of corruption, into glorious liberty, the liberty of the children of God!"[35] The book of Revelation adds the words of Christ, "Behold, I make all things new. . . . And there shall be no more death, neither sorrow, nor crying; neither shall there be any more pain . . . ."[36] Wesley specified some additional particulars: the animals will be restored in vigor, strength, swiftness, understanding, affection, liberty, gentleness, beauty, and "they shall enjoy happiness suited to their state, without alloy, without interruption, and without end."[37]

Conclusion

Such was the ringing conclusion to three centuries of Protestant thought on animal immortality. From the reformer of Wittenberg to the evangelists of England and America, outspoken Protestants affirmed the inestimable and eternal value of *all* of God's created work. They anticipated a joyous eternity for the innocents. They upheld the character of a just and compassionate God. And they based it on Scripture, their sole authority for truth.

35. Romans 8:21.
36. Revelation 21:4, 5.
37. Wesley, *Works*, Vol. VI, 250.

---------- **8** ----------

Scientific Sequels

God created the great creatures of the sea and every living
and moving thing with which the water teems, according
to their kinds, and every winged bird according to its kind.
. . . God blessed them, and . . . God made the wild animals
according to their kinds, the livestock according to their
kinds, and all the creatures that move along the ground
according to their kinds. And God saw that it was good.

—GENESIS 1:21, 25

What Next?

THE OPENING OF PATHS to independent thinking, not only in the
realm of theology but also in the realms of science and philosophy,
was clearly evident in the centuries following the Renaissance, the
Protestant Reformation, New World Explorations, the formation of
the Anglican Church, and other changes during the sixteenth century. This led to a substantial development of ideas pertaining to
animal immortality. Debate and discussion flowed from the pens of
academics and are quite worthy of consideration four centuries later.

René Descartes

Outstanding in the seventeenth century was the eminent French philosopher and scientist René Descartes (1596–1650), famous for his mathematical, or mechanistic, explanation of the universe—and for his teaching that animals are nothing but automata, that is, insensitive material substance. As a faithful Roman Catholic, he intended to strengthen the teachings of the Catholic Church, following Thomas Aquinas in promoting the idea that the distinction between human and animal is the faculty of reason, which must be the spiritual and immortal element in life, inasmuch as matter is incapable of thought.[1] If animals possess any power of reasoning, it would, in Roman Catholic thought, be tantamount to granting them a free will, and thus an immortal soul. But animal instinct precludes both free moral agency and immortality. Further, since a just God would not permit any innocent creature to suffer, the animals (who cannot reason, did not commit sin, and will not be rewarded with heaven) cannot possibly suffer, which means that they have no feeling, and therefore no soul.[2] In Descartes' opinion, Bradford and Calvin were quite wrong.

But Descartes also leveled his arguments against the irreligious libertines who insisted that animals and man must both be immortal or both mortal. Of course, as skeptics, the libertines wanted to prove the mortality of both, for to them immortality was a mirage for people and a farce for animals. They, in fact, anticipated the logical conclusions of Nicolas Malebranche (1638–1715), a priest who tried to reconcile Descartes' ideas with standard Catholic thought, but whose teachings inadvertently spread the notion that animals have no feeling, and ultimately led to the atheistic mechanism that appeared a century later. Descartes and Malebranche would have recoiled in horror from the totally materialistic view of life expressed by physician-philosopher Julien Offray de La Mettrie (1709–51) in his book *L'Homme-Machine*,

---

1. Rosenfield, *Beast-Machine*, 21.
2. Rosenfield, *Beast-Machine*, 47.

but La Mettrie and his followers actually considered Descartes as the originator of their ideas.

Opposition to Cartesianism gained momentum through a type of literature known as "theriophily," meaning admiration for animals, produced by some French philosophes and poets. However, among them only a lesser-known author, Charles Bonnet (1720–93) in *La Palingénésie philosophique* (1769) defended the idea of a future life for animals.[3] Others retained Descartes' mechanistic understanding of animals, while leaving behind his view of discounting animal suffering.

Biblical Authority?

Throughout the centuries of Christian history, the Bible as God's authoritative revelation has been accepted with varying degrees of conviction. It fell to a low point just prior to the Protestant Reformation and reached a peak in the Lutheran, Reformed, and Puritan spheres of influence in Europe and America. For a time, into the early eighteenth century, the Bible was considered of premier value in intellectual circles, but by the end of the nineteenth century its pre-eminence was gone and its prestige was spiraling rapidly downward. To understand how the idea of a future life for animals passed into near oblivion in this period, it is necessary to evaluate what if any part the increase of scientific studies played in this development.

In addition to Descartes, illustrious scholars whose names are frequently and honorably repeated in the annals of science, such as Francis Bacon (1561–1626), Johannes Kepler (1571–1630), and Isaac Newton (1642–1727), intended by their investigations into the world of Nature to bring glory to the God who made it. There was no denial of the sovereign Creator, only a desire to discover how his creation functioned from day to day. Newton had no doubt that empirical facts demonstrated the existence of God,

---

3. Hastings, *Man and Beast*, 230. See also Boas, *Happy Beast*.

and, in fact, that all science was dependent on God.[4] In the next generation, English theologian William Paley (1743–1805) argued for divine purpose and design in created things, and his *Natural Theology* was used as a standard textbook for decades. Seventeenth- and eighteenth-century skepticism belonged rather to the world of philosophy, literature, and politics than to that of science. Most scientists, until the mid-nineteenth century, gave their worship to God whom they recognized as a higher intelligence than themselves and to whom they owed the best fruit of their intellects.

Emanuel Swedenborg

Swedish author and scientist Emanuel Swedenborg (1688–1772) is best known for his founding of the Church of the New Jerusalem, but that facet of his fame was preceded by much scientific research and philosophical contemplation. He served on the Swedish Board of Mines, was a member of the Swedish Parliament, was recognized for his expertise in mechanical engineering, his many inventions, his understanding of such diverse disciplines as astronomy and anatomy, and ultimately his own theological ideas. All of this led to prolific publications of both scientific and ideological tomes, in which he developed his "doctrines" of correspondences, forms, series, degrees, influx, and usefulness.[5] This doctrine of "usefulness" permeated Swedenborg's theology as he held that "all being is created 'from use, in use, and for use' . . .—all of creation exists not just for its own sake but for purposes of the whole."[6] In what is considered his magnum opus, the eight-volume *Arcana Coelestia*, Swedenborg included his consideration of the purpose of animals in the Bible. As he commented verse by verse through the book of Genesis, he stated that "from the Lord through the spiritual world into the subjects of the natural world there is a general influx and

---

4. Burtt, "The Metaphysics of Newton" 131–46.

5. Haller, *Swedenborg's Principles of Usefulness*, xviii–xix.

6. Haller, *Swedenborg's Principles of Usefulness*, xix.

a particular influx"[7] leading to the usefulness of animals. For example, cattle are considered "goods of truth" by which flocks and herds represent interior and exterior goods, while horses, camels, mules, and asses are the intellectual goods.[8] Furthermore, the asses that can be ridden (such as Jesus riding one on Palm Sunday) correspond to "rational truth," while those that carry burdens correspond to "memory knowledges" which he concludes are the "lowest things in man and such as for the most part are put away when the body dies."[9] The logical inference of this trail of thought is that there is no afterlife for animals. Swedenborg is not specific on this point, but the conjunction of science and theology in the mind of this undisputed genius has deeply impacted western society, as John Haller's book *Swedenborg's Principles of Usefulness* shows by its subtitle *Social Reform Thought from the Enlightenment to American Pragmatism.*

The Expansion of Science

Before 1850, European and American universities, weighted toward theology, classical languages, and literature rather than science, prepared the serious student primarily for service in the church. However, the impressive rise of scientific discovery and growing interest in the natural world made, if not always professional scientists, at least competent naturalists of many churchmen. The nineteenth century was the age of the clergyman-naturalist, authors of many volumes, the most famous of which were the Bridgewater Treatises. In 1833 Thomas Chalmers (1780–1848) published his two-volume work, *On the Power, Wisdom, and Goodness of God as Manifested in the Adaptation of External Nature to the Moral and Intellectual Constitution of Man,* and in 1835 William Kirby (1759–1850) published *On the Power, Wisdom, and Goodness of God as Manifested in the Creation of Animals and in Their History, Habits, and Instincts.*

7. Swedenborg, *Arcana*, Vol 8, 4164.

8. Swedenborg, *Arcana*, Vol 8, 4278.

9. Swedenborg, *Arcana*, Vol 8, 5492.

In *Protestants in an Age of Science* (1977), T. D. Bozeman (b. 1942) has shown that during the first half of the nineteenth century, science and theology remained amiable partners in the quest for truth, with the weight of truth given ultimately to theology. Following the empirical approach to science, even the Princeton Presbyterians, on whom Bozeman particularly focuses, adopted "Baconianism," the inductive method, in studying Scripture. In his *Systematic Theology*, Charles Hodge (1797–1878), Princeton professor for fifty-eight years, wrote, "the theologian must be guided by the same rules in the collection of facts, as govern the man of science."[10] As a Scripturalist, Hodge saw no conflict between the Bible and science, for he saw latitude in Scripture and developmental changes in science. He saw as evidence of the divine origin of Scripture that they were written "on such a high level that all the mutations of human science take place beneath them without ever coming into collision with their teachings."[11] Hodge and others—for example, Edward Robinson (1794–1863), Horace Bushnell (1802–76), James Henry Thornwell (1812–62), Philip Schaff (1819–93), W. G. T. Shedd (1820–94)—all hoped to deepen and solidify the union of faith and science, but unfortunately the final third of the century saw their hopes evaporate.[12]

As the century progressed and as the professional scientist superseded the amateur, two areas of scientific investigation unfolded in such a way as to disrupt the prevailing harmony between faith and science and to cast doubt on the veracity of the Bible. One area of study was the earth itself, and before the century was half over, geology had thrown down the gauntlet in the face of the prima facie meaning of Genesis 1.

But the sharpest conflict of the latter half of the century was not so much concerned with geology as with the relation of mankind to the rest of the animal world,[13] and the fundamental question of biology: What is life? Is it biological evolution explained

10. Hodge, *Systematic Theology*, 11.

11. Hodge, *Systematic Theology*, 854.

12. Conser, *God and the Natural World*.

13. Rudwick, "Shape and Meaning of Earth History," 316.

by natural selection? Nineteenth-century biologists and physicians pursued this "great biologic problem" and offered new solutions to the perennial debate.[14] Could life be explained in exclusively materialistic terms or was an invisible "vital force" necessary? Was there actually a dividing line between humans and other animals, between organic and inorganic, between life and death? Chemists, physicists, and philosophers agonized, argued, and added their best analyses in support of vitalism, of mechanism, of the possibility of spiritual quality in life, or of complicated cellular processes only.[15] Much of the debate centered on the biological question of creation by design versus evolution by chance.

Charles Darwin

The name that everyone connects with the popularization of evolutionary biological science is Charles Darwin (1809–82). His Cambridge education prepared him for the church, but the famous voyage of the "Beagle" set the direction of his life firmly on scientific investigation. His research was stimulating, and he plunged into it with the constancy and thoroughness of devoted passion and worked out the theory of natural selection. "No one with an unbiased mind can study any living creature, however humble, without being struck with enthusiasm at its marvelous structure and properties," exclaimed Darwin.[16] Theologian and philosopher Stephen H. Webb, noting that Darwin appreciated even the emotional and trivial aspects of animal life, probably smiled as he wrote, "Simply put, Darwin loved animals."[17] Thus it was that new worlds of knowledge opened before Darwin's eyes and the old world waited with anticipation for him to spread these jewels before them.

Simultaneously with Darwin, but scarcely aware of each other, another British scientist, Alfred Russel Wallace (1823–1913),

14. Haller, "The Great Biologic Problem," 81–88.

15. Haller, "The Great Biologic Problem," 85–86.

16. Darwin, *Origin of Species*, 528.

17. Webb, *On God and Dogs*, 117.

also developed the theory of natural selection.[18] Independently, unknowingly, the two men came up with almost the same scientific explanations for the origin of life, and then worked together for several years. Eventually, however, Wallace began to struggle further to find an explanation for the origin of the intellectual and moral aspects of the human brain. Ultimately he concluded that there must be a "Higher Intelligence" in the whole scheme of life, and he looked for a spiritual solution. As he sought for an answer, he was attracted to an increasingly popular movement known as Spiritualism, whereby seekers received extra-sensory perceptions of the spirit world, and as he delved deeper into spiritual possibilities, he and Darwin parted ways.

Darwin himself experienced some spiritual misgivings, however, since the conclusions that he began to draw from his research obviously brought him into conflict with the Genesis story of creation, especially the statements that God created the animals "according to their kinds"—not on an evolutionary continuum. He did not approach this conflict lightly, and it actually caused him continual anxiety throughout the remainder of his life. By 1850 he had declared himself agnostic, but not until 1859 did he publish his *Origin of Species by Means of Natural Selection* and another dozen years passed before *The Descent of Man* (1871) appeared. The world received both books with tremulous enthusiasm.

Enthusiasm over the theory of evolution has nonetheless had its flipside: the quandary of balancing belief in a loving Creator-God with the apparent agonies of living beings during the evolutionary process. Darwin would have appreciated the deliberations of several twentieth- and twenty-first-century philosophers who have faced this predicament. For instance, Christopher Southgate has examined multiple possibilities, offering an in-depth study of evolutionary theodicy in his masterpiece *The Groaning of Creation.* He does not shy away from the difficulties involved and has done everything possible to come to a satisfying philosophical and biblical conclusion.

18. Haller, *Fictions of Certitude*, 88.

Expanding Interests

Yet another indication of the growing excitement over scientific discoveries in the nineteenth century was the founding of several popular periodicals. *Nature*, specializing in geology and astronomy, first appeared in 1869. *Popular Science Monthly*, established in 1872, addressed primarily the natural sciences, and served to inform the general reader of scientific progress, as well as to provide a forum for professional debate. One of the early debates centered on the continual argument between the classics and the sciences in education. The "Editor's Table," controlled by the pen of Edward Youmans (1821–87), declared that "the study of man is really the most important of all studies, and must always continue to be so," but literature and languages are "incompetent in method, destitute of necessary data."[19] Science provides *the* necessary method of learning "and is as comprehensive as the phenomena of the world we live in. It is not merely knowledge, it is the most perfect form of knowledge, upon all subjects, which it is possible to know." Furthermore, asserted Youmans, "science is the investigator of Truth—truths of all orders, and by all mental operations through which truth can be established."[20]

Establishing truth by scientific investigation triggered some rather amazing experimental gyrations. In his article on "The Great Biologic Problem," historian John S. Haller relates the story of a certain Duncan MacDougall, a Massachusetts physician, who believed that he could prove the material existence of the human soul, or soul-substance, by weighing an individual immediately before and after death. MacDougall believed that the continuation of a conscious personality after death necessitated space-occupying substance, and that weight-loss at death was evidence of "gravitative matter" that left the body and ascended into the earth's ether.[21] After weighing some bodies immediately before and after death, he calculated that the soul weighed three ounces. As you

---

19. Youmans, "Editor's Table," *PSM*, Vol. III, 640.

20. Youmans, "Editor's Table," *PSM*, Vol. III, 639.

21. Haller, "The Great Biologic Problem," 81 and 86.

can imagine, MacDougall's hypothesis did not gain many disciples in the medical community!

Further Conflicts

Pure materialism was the aggressive scientific philosophy of the day. It appeared virtually self-evident to many. As F. W. H. Myers (1843–1901) pointed out in his lecture on "Science and a Future Life" (1893), science had established that "to every mental change some cerebral change corresponds; with the inference that, when the brain decays, the mind is extinct as well."[22] Not only speaking and acting, but even thoughts and emotions correspond to movement in the material substance of the brain. Search for the soul remained fruitless as scientists contended that even Descartes' suggestion for a "seat of the soul," the pineal gland, was a vestige of the eye of some elemental ancestor.[23]

John William Draper, (1811–82), well-loved professor of chemistry at the College of the City of New York, believed that there was no limit to scientific understanding of the world in natural rather than supernatural terms. With his *History of the Conflict between Religion and Science*, Draper more than anyone else elaborated on the ongoing antagonism between what he perceived as the static mindset of faith and the progressive scientific intellect. For Draper, religion symbolized "all claims on the blind devotion of men," whereas science freed them from all "obligation except the honest pursuit of knowledge."[24] His teaching has been applauded by some for "pointing the way" in a crucial stage in one's education, namely, "the means for cutting loose from every species of authoritarianism."[25]

The question of immortality may evoke in the independent mind images of the heavy hand of an authoritarian church. Perhaps

22. Myers, *Science and a Future Life*, 4.
23. Myers, *Science and a Future Life*, 19.
24. Fleming, *Draper*, 93.
25. Fleming, *Draper*, 93.

it was for that reason that the very first issue of the *Popular Science Monthly* included an article entitled "Science and Immortality" by T. W. Fowle (1835–1903), rector of Islip. He saw the belief in immortality as an essential ingredient to religion, a matter of "utmost importance," and pointed out that disbelief in immortality, which was formerly confined to philosophical circles, "is rapidly passing from the few into the popular mind; that it is becoming part of the furniture of the human intellect, and is powerfully influencing the very condition of human nature."[26] He recognized that those who reject immortality will have "no reasonable hope of ever discovering anything about man's future destiny."[27]

Darwin himself avoided writing about anything metaphysical because his field of study was exclusively biological. It is unlikely that he was able to avoid thinking about the intangible and the eternal, however. His wife was quietly concerned for the destiny of his soul, and it bothered him to think that he was upsetting her.[28] It is also hard to imagine that in the grief he suffered over the deaths of three beloved children, he did not meditate on the prospect of immortality. Nevertheless, Darwin felt obligated to lay Scripture aside because he could not reconcile its account of creation with what he saw in the natural world. And although, as theologian Stephen Webb observed, "Darwin would suggest more similarities than differences between animals and humans, the worldview of the sciences tends to subordinate ethical concern to the advancement of knowledge, . . . the exclusive domain of and the reason for the infinite value of humanity alone."[29]

The Problem of Problems: No Conclusion

Many efforts were made during the latter half of the nineteenth century to reconcile Scripture and science, but biologist and

---

26. Fowle, "Science and Immortality," *PSM* Vol. I, 1872, 28.
27. Fowle, "Science and Immortilty," *PSM* Vol. I, 1872, 29.
28. Himmelfarb, *Darwin*, 362–63.
29. Webb, *On God and Dogs*, 105–6.

Congregational minister Newman Smyth (1843–1925) believed that "the problem of problems" facing the scientist and the Christian of his generation remained the frustrating and perhaps unanswerable question: "Is man, through whatever intermediate forms he may have descended, the son of God, or is he the unintended product of molecular forces?"[30] Of course, Darwin had struggled with that very question. In a letter to a friend, he confessed that he had an "inward conviction" that the universe was not the result of mere chance. But he added that "the horrid doubt always arises whether the convictions of man's mind, which has been developed from the mind of the lower animals, are of any value or at all trustworthy. Would anyone trust in the convictions of a monkey's mind," asked Darwin, "if there are any convictions in such a mind?"[31] Perhaps the more fundamental questions are: What is man? What is animal? Is man just a little lower than the angels, as the Psalmist said, or just a little higher than the brutes, as Darwin said?

People have asked these same questions for millennia, but perhaps never was the debate more sharply drawn than in the late nineteenth century. In *Protestant Thought and Natural Science: A Historical Interpretation* (1960), John Dillenberger concluded that the impact of Darwinism, by which the very concept of humanity itself was being challenged, was "the final threat to all the vertical and depth dimension within man and the cosmos." He despaired of the ability of scientists and theologians of the age even to deliberate constructively because Darwinism "marked the culmination of a period in which no adequate symbols were left for expressing and thinking about the classical Christian heritage, . . . one of those rare periods in history in which theology was virtually impossible, when the crisis of language and imagination excluded the essential depth of both God and man."[32] Science had posed a threat to the Christian faith, and had nearly destroyed it.

30. Smyth, *The Religious Feeling*, reviewed in *PSM* Vol. XII, 505.

31. Greene, *Death of Adam*, 336.

32. Dillenberger, *Protestant Thought*, 251. Subsequent to Dillenberger's work is Kaiser's *Creation and the History of Science*, a Christian survey of centuries of scientists, philosophers, and theologians.

9

Romantic Irrationality

He has made everything beautiful in its time.
He has also set eternity in the hearts of men, yet . . .

—ECCLESIASTES 3:11

They exchanged the truth of God for a lie, and worshiped
and served created things rather than the Creator.

—ROMANS 1:25

Loving the Creature

It was not the world of science alone, however, that provoked the dichotomy between faith and knowledge in the nineteenth century mind. Arising from philosophical and literary circles was a second formidable challenge which became known as Romanticism, "whatever it was," as historian Roland Stromberg writes with a scholarly smile.[1] To produce a concise definition of Romanticism would be a Sisyphaean task; volumes of description have scarcely sufficed. But that it altered the course of western history no one denies.

1. Stromberg, *European Intellectual History*, 43.

The philosophical roots of Romanticism can be traced to Immanuel Kant (1724–1804) who, though unquestionably an Enlightenment thinker, rejected certain elements of its thought, opening the way to new ideas. Basically, Enlightenment philosophy had rejected supernatural revelation and human sinfulness and taught the ability of the human mind to understand everything by means of "pure reason." In his *Critique of Pure Reason* (1781), Kant opposed the idea that all knowledge is based on logic, positing instead two realms of knowledge: the scientific, which he described as exact and useful, but superficial; and the religious, which is real and profound, but unattainable. He believed God to be unknowable, either by rational proof or by sense experience, concluding that the dilemma opened the way for some kind of faith, and from there, via intuition, came the channel to romantic thought.

The Pleasure of Romanticism

The literature of the Romantics is unquestionably beautiful. Certainly anyone who has a tender heart will find pleasure in singing . . .

> Flow gently, sweet Afton, among thy green braes!
> Flow gently, I'll sing thee a song in thy praise!

. . . or will smile lovingly in whispering,

> "Little Lamb, who made thee?
> Dost thou know who made thee?
> Gave thee life, and bid thee feed,
> By the stream and o'er the mead;
> Gave thee clothing of delight,
> Softest clothing, wooly, bright;
> Gave thee such a tender voice,
> Making all the vales rejoice?
> Little Lamb, who made thee?
> Dost thou know who made thee?"[2]

---

2. William Blake, *Songs of Innocence*, quoted in Spencer, ed., *British Literature*, Vol. II, 18.

Many authors who are regarded as having established the Romantic movement are still known, loved, and enjoyed in the twenty-first century. From Germany came Johann von Goethe (1749–1832) and Friedrich Schiller (1759–1805); from Scotland, Robert Burns (1759–96); from France, François-René Chateaubriand (1768–1848), Alphonse de Lamartine (1790–1869), Jules Michelet (1798–1874), Victor Hugo (1802–85), and of course, the renowned instigator of it all, Jean-Jacques Rousseau (1712–78) who is described as having catapulted the literary world out of the "cold" rationalism of the Enlightenment into the heated passion of Romanticism.

In England Samuel Taylor Coleridge (1772–1834) and William Blake (1757–1827) created the atmosphere, while Lord Byron (1788–1824), Percy Bysshe Shelley (1792–1822), and John Keats (1795–1821) reveled in the glory of some exquisite moments of the past while achieving some for themselves in the future. And in turning the intellectual tables of the world, William Wordsworth (1770–1850), who encapsulated the romantic's search for life's deepest significance in beauty, in medieval romance, in the emotion of the heart, and above all in nature, exclaimed:

> One impulse from a vernal wood
> may teach you more of man,
> of moral evil and of good
> Than all the sages can.[3]

Whether trees can teach human beings "of moral evil and of good" can be debated, but in any case, there was at that time a rather pronounced emphasis on moral living and an increase in what we term "humanitarianism," which began in the late eighteenth century, and included prison reform, poor relief, improvement of hospitals, the founding of missionary societies, abolition of slavery, and treatment of animals.

Interest in humanitarian issues grew through the writings of Burns who believed in the brotherhood of all creatures, Blake whose mystic love included all sentient beings, and Shelley who

---

3. Wordsworth, "The Tables Turned," *Selected Poems*, 107.

advocated vegetarianism for a variety of reasons. Devoted to reform in industrialism's ugliest hour, Shelley lashed out at the "old, mad, blind, despised, and dying king,"[4] at the army preying with two-edged sword, and at Christless, Godless religion. When he reviled Parliamentary leaders Henry Addington Sidmouth (1757–1844) and Robert Stewart Castlereagh (1769–1822) as "empty ravens, gibbering night-birds, a shark and a dogfish, sick vultures, scorpions, wolves, crows, and vipers," one would scarcely think that he had any affection for the creatures of the earth! Yet he defended innocent animals and vilified mankind in general as the "butcher of creation."[5] Not always consistent in his lifestyle, Shelley adopted vegetarianism only intermittently. Originally, health was the reason, as the "natural method of life" would afford sanity and virtue, while meat-eating would produce gout, madness, and apoplexy. An affluent man himself, Shelley scoffed at the wealthy who "indulged the unnatural craving for dead flesh"[6] and paid for "the greater licence of the privilege, by subjection to supernumery diseases." When contemplating beauty and truth, he felt dismay for slaughtered animals and asked why there would continue "to rise from the earth a chorus of pain, the cries of the creatures who are tortured and slain, to gratify man's needless desires." Shelley was even known to buy crayfish from the street vender in order to have his servant redeposit them in the Thames River!

According to Wordsworth, wisdom and truth also were to be found in an intuitive communion with nature. He exalted the mind of man, which he described as "A thousand times more beautiful than the earth / On which he dwells," but repeatedly (and inconsistently) turned to physical phenomena for evidence and proof of the superiority of tangible Nature over the mind, "the abyss of idealism."[7] Wordsworth believed that there is a happy feeling in all life, including plants and inanimate objects, and that all nature

---

4. Shelley, "England in 1819," quoted in Spencer, ed., *British Literature*, Vol. II, 294.

5. Shelley, *Two Essays*, 442.

6. Shelley, *Vindication of Natural Diet*, 10-12.

7. Thomas, *Wordsworth and Philosophy*, 179–80.

expresses "one supreme Life, Mind, or Mind-like Reality of which lesser lives are constituents."[8] Expressions like this may cause readers to assume a Christian basis in Wordsworth's poetry, but the message is at root anti-Christian, for he arguably "worshiped the creature rather than the Creator."[9] As philosopher William James (1842–1910) later observed, this was "a new sort of religion of Nature, which has entirely displaced Christianity from the thought of a large part of our generation."[10]

Evangelical Christianity

Paralleling Romanticism chronologically was the rise of Christian evangelicalism, of which Wesley's Methodist revivals and the Church of England's Clapham Sect are examples, both of which played no small part in the humanitarian movement. Historian James Turner credits evangelicalism especially as having inspired anti-slavery action, concern for the insane, and kindness to animals.[11] L. C. Hartley (1906–79), biographer of the poet-humanitarian William Cowper (1731–1800), emphasized that "the great spiritual revival, far from relegating animal existence to a negligible position . . . seems to have accepted the dignity of animal life and even to have added weight to the plea for kindness to animals."[12] Hartley contrasted the motive of the evangelicals, namely, that animals are worthy of kindness because they are creatures of God who is concerned for everything in the universe, with that of the "benevolists" (i.e., non-evangelical humanitarians) who felt that animals were worthy of respect because they were links in a perfect chain of being. Breaking the chain was unthinkable, for every link was inherently valuable.

8. Hartshorne, "In Defense of Wordsworth," 81.

9. Romans 1:25.

10. Turner, *Without God*, 254–55.

11. Turner, *Without God*, 89.

12. Hartley, *William Cowper*, 245.

Several individuals deserve mention because of their persistent labor to better the condition of animals. The first chronologically were Cowper and his contemporary Humphry Primatt (fl.1775) who wrote *On the Duty of Mercy to Brute Beasts* (1776), on which numerous other preachers and humanitarians founded their arguments. Richard Martin (1754–1834), philanthropist and member of Parliament from Ireland, worked for about thirty years to achieve legislation in Parliament making cruelty to animals a criminal offense. He was the target of merciless ridicule year after year, but finally in 1822 an animal protection law was passed. In 1824, the Revd. Arthur Broome (fl.1815–31), an Anglican, became the first director of the Society for the Prevention of Cruelty to Animals. A centennial history of the SPCA also singles out for honor Lewis Gompertz (1784–1861) who "saved the Society from extinction in the most difficult period of its existence" and put into practice the teachings of the ancient Hebrews, "which had always—according to the civilization of those early days—cared for animals in their possession."[13]

The Future?

The humanitarian movement was in theory a revival of the Aristotelian concept of the animal soul (sensation) and in practice a positive response to Christian concern. However, focusing on humane treatment in this life, humanitarians had no need to speak to the issue of a future life for animals. In fact, Hartley points out that Cowper stopped short of implying any such possibility and "was not drawn as Wesley was into the dangerous and difficult consideration of the immortality of the brute creation. . . . . He is content with no more intricate doctrine than the commonplace extension of God's personal superintendence over human life to the realm of nature."[14] The "sensitive soul" does not seek an answer

13. Fairholme and Pain, *A Century of Work*, 69.
14. Hartley, *Cowper*, 222–23.

to a Cartesian question, "Do they think?" but rather an Aristotelian question, "Do they feel?"

Concerned for the physical welfare of animals, William Youatt (1776–1847), the veterinary surgeon for the SPCA, wrote a book entitled *The Obligation and Extent of Humanity to Brutes, Principally Considered with Reference to the Domesticated Animals* (1839). He earnestly appealed for the humane treatment of innocent creatures, and reflected on the fact that Richard Martin, the "advocate of the claims of the brute [was] regarded as a fool or a madman, or a compound of both."[15] By 1839, Parliament had responded, but Youatt still lamented that the best theologians and philosophers of the day had not condescended to plead the cause of the animals. Youatt would like to have established the fact that animals have as much right to protection from maltreatment as people do, even though they are "less intelligent, and not immortal." Their susceptibility to pain, in other words, their sensitive soul, qualifies them for kindness. Youatt hoped to win his readers to a consistent practice of "humanity to the brute which is harmonious with the spirit and doctrines of Christianity," especially the "beautiful principle of Christian charity."[16]

Merging Romanticism, Theology, and Science

The application of a scientific paradigm to theology, via Romanticism, was advanced at the popular level by the inspirational work of Lyman Abbott (1835–1922), a Congregational pastor who related evolutionary theory to Scripture. Abbott believed that revelation itself was a product of evolution and that "theology must be modified constantly to keep pace with advancing knowledge and changing social conditions."[17] He applied the principle of evolution to the person and work of Christ as well, explaining Christ's mission as "not merely to show divinity to us, but to evolve the

15. Youatt, *Obligation and Extent*, 2.

16. Youatt, *Obligation and Extent*, 3–4.

17. Brown, *Lyman Abbott*, vii.

latent divinity which he has implanted in us." Divinity evolves out of humanity; what Christ is, mankind is becoming.[18]

If written revelation and the "living revelation" embodied in Christ are both products of evolution, and science is the proprietor of knowledge, it would behoove the scientist to speak to the development of immortality. It was the geologist Joseph LeConte (1823–1901) who made the most intricate explanation of the evolution of body, soul, spirit, divinity, and immortality. According to evolution, attaining a particular goal is not just the completion of one stage, but also the beginning of the next higher stage of development. Through a long process of individuation, "divine energy" manifests itself in the life-force of plants, in the "anima" of animals, and in the self-conscious spirit of humanity, which is capable of separate existence and therefore immortal.[19] But where in the gradual process of evolution, asked LeConte, did the immortal spirit come in? Was it in the germ-cell? at quickening? at birth? when the individual reaches the capacity of abstract thought? LeConte believed that the emergence of *self-consciousness* is actually the birth of the spirit, and it takes place in the human being at age two or three.[20] He explained that as the human spirit pre-existed "in embryo" in animals, slowly developing over eons of time, so the Divine spirit is "in embryo" in humanity, and finally reaches completion in the life of "the Christ." And as the human is a union of animal and spiritual, so the Christ is the union of human and Divine.[21]

LeConte's work sparked the interest of Clark University student Jacob Richard Street, whose 1898 dissertation is entitled "A Genetic Study of Immortality." In it Street cited LeConte and concluded that biological and psychological evolution coordinate at every point. The desire to live, "this tenacious grasp of life," explained Street, "is the earliest psychic element that has contributed

18. Brown, *Lyman Abbott*, 143.

19. LeConte, *Evolution*, 318–19.

20. LeConte, *Evolution*, 317.

21. LeConte, *Evolution*, 361–62.

to the development of faith in continued personal existence after physical death."[22]

Existence After Death?

LeConte began a search and offered explanations for the existence of the soul of living beings. The search continued in *The Genesis and Evolution of the Individual Soul* (1909) written by the Rev. J. O. Bevan, Anglican rector and noted archaeologist, who considered three possibilities for the origin of the soul: self-evolution, special creation by a Higher Being, or derivation from a Universal Expression, an "incarnation of God from eternity."[23] Bevan preferred this last choice, believing that "the soul is immanent from the beginning; from the origin of the first primitive life-cell (even as a bud is immanent in the root); but it is not evidenced in outward and particular manifestation until the evolutionary period is fulfilled."[24]

Choosing from among these possibilities necessitated a re-examination of the Bible, its origin, and interpretations. This was done by several German scholars, the most famous of whom is Julius Wellhausen (1844–1918). Influenced by Romantic thought and eager to explain the Scriptures using scientific methods, these biblical critics questioned and often denied the historical truth of the claims of biblical texts. Their method, known as "the higher criticism," was widely received in academic circles and led to challenging the doctrines of revelation, inspiration, and post-death experience, whether of eternal punishment or eternal bliss. Several possibilities resulted.

There was in this period a growing abandonment of belief in an afterlife for humans, let along embracing one for animals. In this period rather than the afterlife expanding to welcome animals, it faded as a possibility for any creature, humans included.

22. Street, "Genetic Study of Immortality," 29.

23. Strauss, *Life of Jesus*, 780.

24. Bevan, *Genesis and Evolution*, 22.

Some saw the elimination of the soul as a step forward in a movement toward intellectual independence. F. W. Farrar (1831–1903), dean of Canterbury, reflected on such independence in intellectual circles, and observed that "some writers not only glory in expressing a belief that, apart from his body, man has no soul, and no life beyond the grave, . . . but have even arrived at the point of treating with compassionate disdain those who still cling to the traditional belief."[25] In the twenty-first century, such a statement arouses little comment, but it was a shock to Christians in the nineteenth.

Attacks on the authority of Scripture escalated into confrontational assaults at every level, evidenced, for example, by a letter to the editor of *Popular Science Monthly* asking rhetorically, "Have we not reached that stage of enlightenment and that sound policy at which we can safely drop the supernatural from our religion, and relegate it to the cults of less advanced peoples, who still find it necessary to keep that element ingrafted into their theogonies, in order to awe their simple and unintelligent followers?" The author Addison Child advocated eliminating the supernatural from the Bible itself, expunging all that *science proves false*, "leaving a work that men can read without repulse, and the children in our public schools without pollution."[26]

However, many in this period continued to hold on to the hope for an afterlife taught in Scripture, though disagreements over its nature increased. Some maintained the traditional view of everlasting bliss or torment. Alongside that, a small but growing opinion was universalism, which teaches the ultimate well-being of every individual. Another was that God could continue to seek the sinner after death, even if some may ultimately be lost. A third was annihilationism, or "conditional immortality" in which totally wicked individuals were exterminated while "good" people would survive in some kind of paradise or heaven. Yet with all these different views growing alongside one another, most still did not stop to consider whether or not animals might be included in an afterlife.

25. Farrar, *What Heaven Is*, 1.
26. Child, "Vitiated Moral Teaching," 408.

Conclusion

During the nineteenth century, Scripture, which up to that point had prevailed in the Protestant world as sole authority for faith and life, faced monumental challenges in the form of the natural sciences and philosophical Romanticism. In the post-Darwinian years, Christians had to face these problems and either adjust their theology or entrench and defend a traditional position. Adjustments in theology led to a range of possibilities including modern Christian liberalism, philosophies inspired by oriental religions, and agnosticism. Defense of orthodoxy involved elaborating on the doctrine of verbal inspiration, examining eschatology, and re-affirming the entire concept of supernaturalism and immortality.

If no such reality as "soul" even exists, the discussion is over. But it wasn't! Speculation on the existence of both human and animal soul continued to appear as points of interest in ongoing discussions of evolution. In those Christian circles where the veracity of the Bible was affirmed but evolution was rejected, the challenge was to show a valid and plausible separation between animals and humankind. This requires a closer inspection of the teaching of evangelical Christians and an attempt to explain why they departed from the precepts of some of their forerunners in the faith by emphasizing the existence of the *soul* as the *essential distinction* between human and non-human.

Fundamental Faith

And you also were included in Christ when you heard
the word of truth, the gospel of your salvation.

—EPHESIANS 1:13

Opposition, Orthodoxy, and Omissions

THE COLORFUL INTELLECTUAL THEATRE of the nineteenth century gave its Oscars to Jules Michelet and Charles Darwin and its Emmys to Ralph Waldo Emerson and Thomas H. Huxley, but incorporated in the intriguing thought of these men and their followers lay the crucial elements that became the adversaries of scriptural Christianity. Subjective-romantic criticism and theories of science captured the minds of scholars and challenged the very foundation of Protestant thought: the revealed, written Word of God. Many people who were interested in the subject of the soul either drifted away from scriptural moorings or redefined the Bible in order to correspond to scientific investigation. Alarmed by the impact of these trends, some Christians who adhered to the authority of Scripture attempted to fully defend and explain their beliefs, and, in so doing, gave rise to the movement known as Christian Fundamentalism.

Fundamentalism

As discussion developed, there were four groups who identified themselves as fundamentalists: the Keswick Convention, the Conferences for Bible Prophecy, the Princeton Presbyterians, and the authors of the twelve-volume *Fundamentals of the Faith*. There are specific distinctions among the four groups that are important in church history, so it is not accurate to view fundamentalism as a monolithic movement, yet all four strands stood together against the opposition.

The burden of their efforts fell into two spheres: first, the defense of Scripture as the sole and inerrant source of truth, and, secondly, the doctrines of soteriology (salvation) and of eschatology (future, end times). Both of these major issues implicate belief about animal immortality and if it can be shown that Scripture is trustworthy and that it teaches the immortality of all living creatures, then fundamentalists should have been the most vocal in defending eternal life for non-human beings; and in addition, if a substantial heavenly existence includes animals, some distinction other than "soul" or "immortality" must define *homo sapiens*.

Their defense of Scriptural authenticity and their interpretations of eschatology require some clarification before any explanation of their views on animal immortality can be understood.

Attacks against the Inerrancy of Scripture

The most devastating attack on fundamentalist belief in the inerrancy of Scripture came from academic studies in "the higher criticism," that is, the endeavor to examine biblical texts—their origins (dates, authorship, sources, styles, etc.) and claims—on the same historical terms as any ancient text, granting them no special treatment as inspired Scripture. Julius Wellhausen, as noted before, is the best-known of the higher critics, and his scholarship "gave him a place in biblical studies comparable to that of Darwin in biology."[1] The encroaching effects of doubt as to biblical inerrancy because of the higher criticism became quite obvious in American Christianity shortly after the Civil War.

Another competitor to the doctrine of biblical inerrancy was subjective intuition, or testing Scripture "by the oracle God places in the breast," as expressed by the Unitarian leader Theodore Parker (1810–60). According to him, the Bible must become "the servant and not the master of Christians."[2]

A further attack appeared in *Lectures on Natural Theology* (1867), by educator and naturalist Paul A. Chadbourne (1823–83) who wrote, "We are not yet prepared to pronounce the Bible obsolete, . . . but we freely acknowledge that the Bible must stand the tests which science can fairly put it to."[3] Chadbourne believed that it made no difference to one's belief in the character of God whether God created the species separately or let them evolve naturally from one microscopic germ.[4]

To a fundamentalist, however, science was not actually the basic issue; it was the character of God himself that was at stake. It matters, they said, whether God has revealed truth or falsehood. The scientist Joseph LeConte had held that the test of truth is reason, inasmuch as divine truth "filtering through man's mind must take imperfections characteristic of the man and of the age." Apparently assuming that humanity's power of reason is unimpaired, he warned that revelation "must be redistilled in the alembic of reason to separate the divine truth from the earthly impurities."[5]

Further opinion on that idea came from Howard Crosby (1826–91), chancellor of the University of the City of New York, who wrote in *The Fundamentals*, "In these days when so much is made of science, let them [i.e. preachers] leave science alone. All

1. Douglas et al., eds., *New International Dictionary*, 1033.

2. Brown, *Rise of Biblical Criticism*, 161, quoting Theodore Parker.

3. Chadbourne, *Lectures*, 23.

4. Chadbourne, *Lectures*, 172–73.

5. LeConte, *Evolution*, 333–34.

the knowledge of the material world, which science deals in, has nothing to do with the soul's salvation. That is in a different sphere altogether."[6] He continued, "Science is merely the study of matter, an examination into natural sequences; but what has that to do with man's immortal soul . . . ?"[7]

Fundamentalist Responses

To strengthen believers in the face of these theological opponents, several leaders in the fundamentalist movement organized Bible Conferences that were held annually for many years. Each conference lasted approximately a week, with five sermons each day, described not as eloquent orations but as "a plain story" told "in a plain manner."[8] The emphasis on the sufficiency of Scripture was abundantly clear, as evidenced in explaining the success of the conferences, "not by exciting exhortations nor by learned discourses, nor by new and startling themes, but by simple Bible-readings, in which the Sacred Scriptures have been their own interpreter."[9]

Unflinchingly firm in their defense of Scripture also were the Presbyterian professors at Princeton Seminary. Though few in number, these men exerted steady influence for over a century, from the inception of the Seminary in 1811 until the official repudiation of scriptural inerrancy through the Auburn Affirmation of 1924. Archibald Alexander (1772–1851) and his son Joseph A. Alexander (1809–60), Charles Hodge (1797–1878) and his son Archibald A. Hodge (1823–86), Benjamin B. Warfield (1851–1921), and Francis L. Patton (1843–1932) are the most familiar names. Intellectual stature combined with single-minded and inter-generational dedication to the Seminary (three generations of Hodges, in fact) built a citadel of orthodoxy against the mounting pressures of the higher criticism and modernism, and their voluminous

6. Crosby, *The Fundamentals,* Vol. III, 176.

7. Crosby, *The Fundamentals,* Vol. III, 177.

8. Sandeen, *Roots of Fundamentalism,* 137.

9. Sandeen, *Roots of Fundamentalism,* 138.

manuscripts undergirded the entire fundamentalist movement with academic credibility. Charles Hodge's *Systematic Theology* (1873) probably wielded the most influence over the many students who took up pastorates throughout the nation, while Joseph Alexander's commentaries, A. A. Hodge's *Outlines of Theology* (1860) and *Popular Lectures on Theological Themes* (1887), and Warfield's New Testament studies, plus his posthumously published *Revelation and Inspiration* (1927–32) and *Perfectionism* (1927) maintained a stabilizing effect in theological controversies.

With a clear-cut legacy from such documents as the French Confession of 1559, the Belgic Confession of 1561, and the Second Helvetic Confession of 1566, which declared, "We believe and confess the canonical Scriptures of the holy prophets and apostles of both Testaments to be the true Word of God, and to have sufficient authority of themselves, not of men . . ."[10] it cannot be asserted that these fundamentalists were creating any new doctrine, but rather defending the authority, inspiration, and inerrancy of Scripture, adding to a long history of belief that God has revealed *truth*.[11]

Soteriology and Eschatology

The doctrine of salvation as a gift of God through the atonement of Christ also came under attack. Earning one's way to heaven by the fulfillment of a variety of moral requirements became increasingly popular, perhaps because of the effects of the Victorian age of propriety and morality (including humanitarianism) or as a parallel to American individualism and self-responsibility. In any case, many Christians turned away from belief in salvation "by grace through faith alone" and taught some form of salvation by works. De-emphasizing even the necessity of eternal salvation, they focused on societal problems that were becoming increasingly evident and could be addressed through a "social gospel." They lamented that

10. Cochrane, *Reformed Confessions*, 224.

11. Refer to footnote 17 for an explanation of several views of biblical interpretation.

forgiveness of sin would not improve tenement housing, and furthermore, heaven was too remote.

The apparent irrelevance of a heavenly future, which seemed so far away was, however, connected to doctrines of an earthly eschatology, several varieties of which became topics of exciting conversation. Most prominent were three interpretations of passages in the books of Daniel, Thessalonians, and Revelation, dealing with the return of Christ and with a peaceful "millennium," the thousand-year period described in Revelation 20:1–6: first, premillennialism, which teaches a soon return of Christ with its ensuing happy thousand years; secondly, postmillennialism, which postpones the return of Christ until after the peaceful millennium, relegating the final blessed future to an exceedingly distant time; and thirdly, amillennialism, which considers the "thousand years" of Revelation 20 as a symbolic way of referring to the present time between Christ's resurrection victory over Satan and his second coming.

Many Christians who did not want to fall into the works-salvation of the social gospel, yet wanted to meet the needs of the poor, felt somehow obligated to explain this millennium and its accompanying and perplexing period of tribulation spoken of in Daniel 9 and Matthew 24, and focused instead on a "rapture" which would take people out of this present evil world. Although they could not agree on whether this rapture would occur before a fore-warned tribulation, during it, or after it, these fascinating details captured the imagination of the majority of American fundamentalists to the extent that many fixed their hopes on the rapture and the millennium rather than on eternity.

To these fundamentalists, the events of the "end times" were easily describable. The rapture would be a physical, though secret, exit from this world; the tribulation would be a physical, visible, and miserable (but brief) actuality in this world; the millennium (in some ways a parallel to the social gospel's dream of a perfected society) would be the physical, visible, peaceful reign of Christ the King in this world; the return of Christ would be a physical, visible, and exhilarating moment when "every eye will see him";

and the battle of Armageddon and the final judgment would be the physical, visible, and cataclysmic events that would terminate time. "The drama of the future" in fundamentalist eschatology, explain authors Colleen McDannell and Bernhard Lang in *Heaven: A History*, "is decidedly this-worldly; it occurs during the period before and during the millennium, not in a heavenly world."[12]

Because the anticipated earthly millennium would be glorious, attention turned to biblical descriptions of this era to come—and these descriptions certainly included non-human creatures. Animals (and plants) will be just as much a part of the millennial world as of the present one, and they, along with Jews and Gentiles, believers and unbelievers, will all live together under the benevolent rule of Jesus Christ. According to Isaiah 11, 35, and 65, gladness and joy will replace sorrow and sighing, blind eyes and deaf ears will be opened, everyone will live at least a hundred years, vineyards will produce abundantly, people will beat their swords into plowshares and their spears into pruning hooks, and there will be no war.[13] Universal peace will prevail for a thousand years. By the end of the nineteenth century, the concept of the "peaceable kingdom" had already become somewhat fashionable, popularized through art as well as preaching. Even today, people still love the works of artist Edward Hicks (1780–1849), who painted numerous versions of the lion and the lamb relaxing peacefully together, some including little groups of Quakers carrying banners or standing quietly in a corner of the picture.[14] The millennium is beautiful.

Heaven?

While fundamentalists agreed that there would at least *be* a millennium on earth, and that animals would participate in it, the possibility of animals in the far-off heaven remained a problem. Correspondingly, the artistic depictions of heaven that were

---

12. McDannell and Lang, *Heaven: A History*, 352.

13. Isaiah 35; 65; Micah 4.

14. Dillenberger and Taylor, *The Hand and the Spirit*, 88–93.

cautiously offered were few and far between and much less attrac-
tive than those of the millennial "peaceable kingdom." In *The Doré
Bible Illustrations*, Gustav Doré (1832–83) offered only one picture
of the "New Jerusalem," showing a thickly walled city perched on
a mountain of rock with a bottomless chasm dividing it from a
higher mountain of rock on which stand two angels. Even though
the sun is shining through a break in the clouds, the city looks
very grim. There are no windows in the wall, just a few of the nor-
mal peepholes through which medieval bowmen launched their
arrows. Another artist pictured the heavenly Jerusalem as a beau-
tifully walled pyramid with countless houses of translucent gold
building up to the apex where stood the throne of God. However,
in contrast to a millennial picture replete with people, animals, and
plants, heaven appears totally empty. And considering the beautiful descriptions of heaven given by Martin Bucer and John Wesley
in years past, the fundamentalist view was unappealing and caused
many to turn to a more abstract concept of eternity.

The book that unfolds most broadly the conceptions of the
late nineteenth century pertaining to an eternal afterlife is an
anthology entitled *The Home Beyond, or Views of Heaven, and
Its Relation to Earth* (1884). Edited by the Revd. Samuel Fallows
(1835–1922), it includes excerpts from the writings of Dwight L.
Moody, Charles H. Spurgeon, Thomas DeWitt Talmage (1832–
1902), and "400 Other Prominent Thinkers and Writers," many
of whom, though not all, were fundamentalists. The book's 512
pages are full of descriptions of dying moments, heaven, reunions
of families, the ministry of angels, resurrection, and immortality.
Descriptive detail abounds in *The Home Beyond*, including emphasis on the *societal nature* of eternal life, but there is virtually
no mention of the *natural world* at all. It might even seem that
both God and his creation had totally disappeared, and while fundamentalists would certainly object to the disappearance of God,
they could dispense with the rest of the universe without qualms.
One purpose of the natural world in the first place, according to
Romans 1:20, had been to manifest God's invisible qualities, which

indeed it had done and therefore it would no longer be needed.[15] God had created the universe also for the benefit of humankind, and having served that purpose too, it was to be dispensed with in the eschaton. In humanity's future spiritual habitat, material elements would be useless.

Further persuasion to the pre-millennial fundamentalist was the biblical evidence that the heavens and earth are "reserved unto fire," that "the elements shall melt with fervent heat, the earth also and the works that are therein shall be burned up."[16] A theology of that which will be destroyed—the natural world—would be superfluous; and in spite of passages that affirm restoration and renewal for the cosmos, the conflagration after the millennium, to the fundamentalist mind, spells finality for the natural world.

De-materializing heaven has been evident whenever Christianity has been influenced by recurring forms of Gnosticism (cf. some forms of contemporary "New Age" spirituality), by abstractions of the Platonic mind, by mysticism, or by deliberations of whether heaven is a "place" or a "state of being." It is striking that preoccupation with philosophical theology, the social gospel, or the millennium leads to a shifting away from belief in a tangible eternity, the understanding of which in the early twentieth century grew ever less clear.

Back to Animals on Earth

One of the most important works of Christian scholars of the early twentieth century was *The International Standard Bible Encyclopedia* published in 1915. Its preface explains its international attribute, with authors from at least a dozen countries as well as a wide variety of church affiliations. The "general attitude" of the authors is described as that of "reasonable conservatism, . . . acknowledging the rights of a reverent Old Testament criticism" but (in referring to the higher criticism) differing "either in declining

15. Bettex, "The Bible and Modern Criticism," *The Fundamentals*, Vol. I, 78.

16. 2 Peter 3:7–13.

to accept the views of, or in adopting a more cautious attitude toward the advanced Wellhausen school."[17] One can be fairly well-assured that the entries in this encyclopedia were written from the perspective of people who affirm biblical authority.

On the topic of animals, but showing a lack of interest in them, one example in this encyclopedia is the article about Balaam, who had been asked by the king of Moab to curse the Israelites.[18] Although God permitted Balaam to go to Moab, he was halted on the way by an angel with sword in hand. Balaam did not see the angel, but his donkey did, attempted to protect Balaam by refusing to proceed along the road, thereby incurring Balaam's wrath and three beatings, and finally asking Balaam why he deserved the beatings. In discussing this strange conversation, the *ISBE* author wrote merely, "By influencing the soul of Balaam, God caused him to interpret correctly the inarticulate sounds of the animal."[19] That is the extent of the commentary pertaining to the donkey, even though the article fills several columns of print!

It is instructive in studying the progress and regress of biblical interpretation to compare this with the more reformational view of Matthew Henry in his 1706 *Commentary on the Whole Bible*. With vocabulary that sounds rather antiquated to our twenty-first-century ears, Henry wrote, "The righteous God will not see the meanest and weakest abused; but either they shall be enabled to speak in their own defence or he will some way or other speak for them. . . . The ass reasoned with him [i.e., Balaam]; God enabled not only a dumb creature to speak, but a dull creature to speak to the purpose."[20] Henry may not have had a very high opinion of donkeys in general, but he did not deny the actual audible words that this donkey spoke.

17. *ISBE*, Vol. 1, viii. The Wellhausen School declared the Pentateuch to be not the work of Moses but the output of at least four authors (referred to as J, E, D, and P), all from times much later than Moses and separated from each other by hundreds of years. Thus they claimed that the Pentateuch is a patchwork of various earlier documents, offering conflicting accounts of the same stories.

18. Numbers 22–24.

19. *ISBE*, Vol. I, 379.

20. Henry, *One-Volume Commentary*, 166.

A less well-known book appeared in 1903, dedicated to the SPCA, the Humane Association, the Humane Education Society, and eleven other organizations devoted to the protection of animals. Its author was a medical doctor; its title, surprisingly, *The Immortality of Animals.* Dr. E. D. Buckner (1844–1907) drew from theology, history, and science in support of the idea, pointing out that "there is a current of thought from the beginning to the end of the Bible which either expresses or implies that animals share with man immortal life,"[21] that "the doctrine of the immortality of animals was maintained by many Jewish writers and a long list of ancient Christian writers,"[22] and that, among scientists, at least Louis Agassiz "was a firm believer in some future life for lower animals."[23] Buckner began his book by showing that the Hebrew words for "creature," "living soul," "breath of life," and "spirit" all demonstrate the equality of man and beast, and that "perish" in no way means "annihilate." He then reiterated the observations of other authors concerning the mercy of God over his creatures, and emphasized God's communication with animals, notably Balaam's donkey, the ravens who fed Elijah, the fish who swallowed Jonah, and the lions who did not eat Daniel. "It is claimed by the Church," wrote Buckner, "that man is immortal because he can communicate with God. We take the same Bible and prove that God communicated with lower animals, which would indicate a divine nature in them for the same reason."[24] This book exhibits a calm and reasonable attitude on the part of the author, and the reader may wonder why it apparently did not exert a greater impact on either the scientific or the Christian community. Perhaps it was ignored by the one because of its rejection of evolution and by the other because it includes scientific information in its arguments. Fundamentalists from the 1850s on simply had trouble with how to handle the natural world, especially animals, whether from a biblical or a scientific point of view, whether in this life or the next.

21. Buckner, *Immortality of Animals*, 74.
22. Buckner, *Immortality of Animals*, 88.
23. Buckner, *Immortality of Animals*, 80.
24. Buckner, *Immortality of Animals*, 110–11.

Conclusion

Trouble or not, fundamentalists remained united in maintaining the infallibility of Scripture, as truth from the One holy and truth-revealing God. They were also united in affirming the unique position of humankind in God's order of creation and in opposing Darwinism's biological continuity of all life. Revelatory of this opposition are statements of dismay such as, "When you read what some writers say about man and his bestial origin your shoulders unconsciously droop; your head hangs down; your heart feels sick."[25] Unfortunately this also discloses a low esteem of nature, especially of animals.

Though admitting that mankind has much in common with animals, various articles in *The Home Beyond* specify not only the superiority of the human being in matters of mind, conscience, speech, morals, and religion, but state that man "differs absolutely" from the brute beasts.[26] And, in differing "absolutely" from the human being, animals were left with no soul and no immortality. The implication and eventual conclusion could be that, in spite of what God said, his creation may *not* be "very good," and that to spend eternity with animals is non-scriptural, non-spiritual, and probably repulsive.

Bible-believing Christians must be thankful that their forebears defended the truth of Scripture but should recognize, sadly, their failure to produce a thorough theology of the natural world. It is high time to "un-mute" the silence and to honor the One who created, loves, and provides for cattle and coneys alike! Enjoy Psalm 104!

25. Hague, "The Doctrinal Value of the First Chapters of Genesis." *The Fundamentals*, Vol. I, 280.

26. Fallows, *The Home Beyond*, 40–44.

— 11 —

Contemporary Cogitations

Where is the wise man? Where is the scholar?
Where is the philosopher of this age?

—1 CORINTHIANS 1:20

Conversation Continues

IN THE YEARS THAT have elapsed since the thinkers of the nineteenth century "folded the draperies of their couches about themselves and lay down to pleasant dreams," what has become of the idea of immortality? Have we come full circle? Is there agreement on what is meant by soul? Immortality? Self-awareness? Personality? No, debate continues. More ideas. More terms. New words and complicated concepts that demand definition! And still no full theology of the natural world.

Defying Definition: Cosmic Christ

One term that has been used in such discussions during the twentieth century is "cosmic Christ," which originally suggested simply an intimate awareness of the universe. But in the writings of the Jesuit missionary and paleontologist Pierre Teilhard de Chardin (1881–1955), it carried far deeper and more devotional meaning, since he applied the salutary effects of Christ's life and work to the universe. "Lord Jesus," he prayed, "you are the centre towards which all things are moving: if it be possible, make a place for us all [among those] whom your loving care has liberated . . . from the chaos of our present existence and who now are being slowly incorporated into you in the unity of the new earth."[1]

The slow incorporation of all things into a metaphysical unity—the "evolutionary mystique"—was the foundation for Teilhard's scientific and theological views, for he believed that the study of the soul belongs to the field of natural science.[2] Through his alliance of scientific and spiritual evolution, he developed the idea of a process of "hominization" in which the human, unlike an animal, becomes conscious that he or she is conscious. At the convergence of space and time, mankind will reach the "Omega Point," or the "Christ-Omega," which then consumes space and time in a synthesis of love. Christ is the culmination of all things, and the "Christified world [is] a whole that has itself become a person."[3] In his optimistic conception of the future, the entire universe, including death, will be "hominized"; and "by the grace of death, like a continuous exhalation, 'souls' break away, carrying upward their incommunicable loads of consciousness, which, under the synthesizing action of Omega, become immersed in the personal union with the psychic substance of this divine principle of ultimate attraction . . . ."[4] For Teilhard, evolution progresses beyond human self-consciousness toward the idea of the "cosmic Christ," and reaches its ultimate objective when "God shall be all in all."[5]

1. de Chardin, *Hymn of the Universe*, 76.

2. Wildiers, *The Theologian and His Universe*, 191.

3. Wildiers, *The Theologian and His Universe*, 209.

4. Hughes, ed., *Creative Minds*, 427.

5. 1 Corinthians 15:28. See also DeWitt in Hughes, *Creative Minds*, 443. DeWitt's conclusion is that in Teilhard's attempt to unify everything, he "loses

Most heirs of nineteenth-century fundamentalism do not believe in a "cosmic Christ" in Teilhard's sense of the term, but many of them have also "solved" the dilemma of matter vs. spirit by almost effacing matter. For example, like earlier revivalists, some within the grassroots charismatic movement focus on the reality of the Spirit of God and emphasize the crucial (nearly exclusive) role of human emotion in salvation, assurance, and faith for all eventualities of this life. Little attention is given, however, to the resurrection of the body and even less to the destiny of the natural world.

Defying Definition: Cosmic Redemption

The phrase "cosmic redemption" has appeared in some Christian literature, both liberal and evangelical, but it usually implies ecological responsibility rather than the ultimate removal of the post-Edenic curse on creation.[6] One European scholar who writes from a fully biblical standpoint (though not entirely evangelical) uses "cosmic redemption" in an eschatological sense. Oscar Cullmann (1902–99), professor of theology at the University of Basel and the Sorbonne, spoke of this cosmic redemption and pointedly confronted the dichotomy of matter vs. spirit (and thus the gnostic heresy) when he gave the Ingersoll lecture in 1955.[7] His address, "Immortality of the Soul or Resurrection of the Dead? The Witness of the New Testament," argued that the phrase "immortality of the soul" reflects the Greek idea that the body is evil (or, at least, inferior to the soul). Greek immortality offers an afterlife that is a vague, immaterial eternity, while "resurrection of the dead" reflects the Christian idea that the body is not a "prison" from which one

---

himself in a gnosticist speculation," and problems are resolved only at the expense of the tangible.

6. DeWitt, *The Environment and the Christian.*

7. An aside of interest pertaining to the Ingersoll Lecture series, which began at Harvard in the 1890s, is that the 1904 lecture was entitled "Science and Immortality." According to the speaker, Dr. William Osler, "immortality is a complex problem, difficult to talk about, still more difficult to write upon with any measure of intelligence or consistency" (Osler, Science and Immortality, 43). He has certainly been proven correct in that opinion!

escapes at death, but a "temple" that will be restored.[8] Although Cullmann did not specifically make any reference to animals, his affirmation that the Christian faith is set "within the framework of cosmic redemption" implies a wider concept than simply an immaterial eternity.

Defying Definition: A Wide Spectrum

Not surprisingly in the twentieth-century world, Romanticism continued to give its own measure of comfort and a "feeling" of security as people, Christian or not, dealt with the death of their faithful non-human companions. Many examples could be given, but one of special interest comes not from a theological tome but from the diary of an Alaskan musher, that is, one who drives sled dogs. In 1925, a fierce plague suddenly hit the city of Nome and people were dying within hours. Immediate vaccine was essential, but airplanes were not yet equipped to fly in Alaska's -85 degree temperature. Of Norwegian descent, Leonhard Seppala (1878–1967) became one of the heroes of the "Nome Serum Run of 1925" when he and his amazingly persistent dog Togo covered almost twice as many miles as the other hardy teams, making it possible to deliver the vaccine much more quickly than expected. Several decades later, shortly before his own death, Seppala expressed sentiment reflective of Romantic authors as he wrote, "When I come to the end of the trail, I feel that along with my many friends, Togo will be waiting."[9] Immortality is a tender-hearted assumption.

From a different perspective, though also writing with humble intelligence, a background of reformed theology, and basing his argument on human moral consciousness, Professor Loraine Boettner (1901–90) stated that the "difference between men and animals is such that the immortality of the former would seem to exclude that of the latter." Although Boettner admitted that Romans 8 gives warrant for the presence of plants and animals in

8. Cullmann, *Immortality of the Soul or Resurrection of the Dead?* 9, 28, 30.

9. Quoted in Wertheim, "The 1925 Nome Serum Run,"

eternity, he thought that "the *individual* ones that we have known will not be there."[10]

Another author of reformed persuasion, the justifiably well-respected and loved theologian J. O. Buswell, conceded that animals have a soul, mind, and spirit, but concluded even so that because they were not created in the *image* of God "there is no reason to suppose that they have any kind of immortality."[11] Also within the camp of reformed theology, R. C. Sproul agrees that animals are not made in the *image* of God, but points out further that Scripture does not state explicitly that animals do *not* have souls, and therefore the Bible gives us "some reason to hope that departed animals will be restored" (which may imply that Sproul and Buswell do not have the same definition of *soul*), but "we can't know for sure" and proposing an afterlife for animals is "sheer speculation."[12] Calvin, Butler, and Wesley are probably in heaven discussing these issues quite graciously with Boettner, Buswell, and Sproul right now—as well as with the ever-beloved author of the Narnia books, C. S. Lewis (1898–1963), who wrote that "Christians may justly hesitate to suppose any beasts immortal," warning that we "must not think of a beast by itself, and call that a personality and then inquire whether God will raise and bless *that*."[13] Bucer and Bradford would disagree. They fully expected to recognize individual animals at the final resurrection and will smile at Lewis's shock—and joy!

There are other authors of various theological positions who have added their expertise to the issue. Gary Kowalski, a minister in the Unitarian Universalist Society, poses and contemplates twelve intriguing questions in his book *The Souls of Animals*, such as, "Do animals have a sense of the mysterious?" "Why do birds sing?" "Are animals conscious of themselves?" In the thought-provoking chapter "Do animals know right from wrong?" Kowalski deals with the definition of morality and gives evidence of altruistic behavior on

10. Boettner, *Immortality*, 85–86.

11. Buswell, *Systematic Theology*, 242.

12. Sproul, *Now That's a Good Question*, 290–91.

13. Lewis, *The Problem of Pain*, 139–41.

the part of several species of animals. While recognizing that animals have differing loyalties and sympathies, he attributes to animals an ethical sense shown in their interaction with one another. There is a lot in Kowalski's book that an orthodox Christian can agree with, but in defining "soul" as "the magic of life," he focused on the here and now, and avoided the issue of eternity.[14]

Another author with undeniably exquisite literary style, Sy Montgomery has penned twenty books, one of which is the fascinating *Soul of an Octopus*. In it, she delineates the intricacy of the personality and intelligence of octopuses, their friendship with human beings, and their soul. Listing a dozen or so definitions of the soul, she ultimately concludes that if she herself has a soul, so does the octopus.[15]

Probing the unique personality of canines, Lutheran seminary professor Andrew Root believes that dogs are the only animals who communicate with humans via eye contact. Looking face-to-face, eye-to-eye, the dog can express his desires to his master or his concern for the master's well-being. Thus, from eye to face to communication to compassion to soul, Root analyzes the psychology of the bonding of human and dog, a spiritual connection stretching from earth to eternity.[16] It is rather disconcerting that Root does not base his expectation of animal presence in heaven on Scripture itself. From a psychological and emotional viewpoint, and feeling one's way "into reality," he holds "a theological conviction by faith" that his dog will be resurrected. Yet does he *really* believe that he will see his pet again? His answer is "tentative," though because love and grace are eternal, he concludes that the "love of a dog is strong enough to last both in this world and the next."[17]

With a tender heart, much research, and steadfast adherence to biblical truth, Mary Buddemeyer-Porter entitled one of her books *Animals, Immortal Beings*, a survey of relevant Scripture

14. Kowalski, *The Souls of Animals*, 142.

15. Montgomery, *Soul of an Octopus*, 228.

16. Root, *Grace of Dogs*, 135.

17. Root, *Grace of Dogs*, 140.

passages highlighted with commentary. Citing works from such widely differing theologians as St. Bonaventure (1217–74), John Calvin, and many others, she encapsulates the Christian expectation of the presence of all animals (individual personalities, domestic and wild) in heaven for eternity. Bucer and Wesley would be justifiably pleased.

Satisfaction or Sorrow?

Reminiscent of Descartes and other mechanistic adherents, a predominant secular philosophy that Christians of all varieties face is materialism, an important axiom for much scientific research. Scientific experiments have been wonderful, fascinating, and satisfying! But for materialists, spirit, soul, immortality, and eternity do not fit into their categories, so might as well not exist. And so, when faced with death, many materialists undoubtedly could agree with William Cullen Bryant (1749–1878) who wrote:

> Earth, that nourished thee, shall claim
> Thy growth, to be resolved to earth again,
> And, lost each human trace, surrendering up
> Thine individual being, shalt thou go
> To mix forever with the elements,
> To be a brother to the insensible rock
> And to the sluggish clod . . . .[18]

Although Bryant undoubtedly intended to comfort his readers as death grants the equality of everyone in "the great tomb of man," the poem nonetheless does reflect a hopeless materialism.

An additional and overriding legacy of the nineteenth century, so very evident in the twentieth, and continuing to the present, is that of plain and pervasive disbelief in the truth of the Bible itself. The brilliant non-Christian philosopher Ludwig Feuerbach (1804–72) rejected biblical truth, but praised Martin Luther—because Luther permitted his son Paul to study medicine and "so be

18. Bryant, "Thanatopsis," 109.

in a position to deny the immortality of the human soul."[19] Immortality, as well as God, according to Feuerbach, exists only in the feeling of the human heart, while a "real, external, objective immortality . . . is the source of delusion."[20] Feuerbach's atheism and materialism laid philosophical foundations that have had earth-shaking repercussions in every field of study and walk of life. In contemporary secular academia, there is no discipline—humanities, sciences, fine arts, or whatever—that considers its purpose to be that of bringing glory to God.

It is not a surprise to note that the speaker at Harvard's 1961 Ingersoll lecture, Hans Jonas (1903–93), a historian of religion, said that "the modern temper is uncongenial to the idea of immortality." Jonas did not believe that there is any individualized, conscious life after death; we human beings have "taken our lonely stand in time between the twofold nothing of before and after."[21] Obviation of God in the educational world is nearly ubiquitous. Immortality has become an illusion, a fairy tale, or a lie. Sadly, many agree with the German poet, Bertolt Brecht (1898–1956), who wrote:

> Do not be misled!
> There is no return.
> Day goes out at the door;
> You might feel the night wind:
> There is no tomorrow . . . .
> Do not be misled
> To drudgery and wasting disease!
> What fear can still touch you?
> You die like all the animals
> And nothing comes after.[22]

19. Küng, *Eternal Life?*, 7.

20. Feuerbach, *The Essence of Christianity*, 285.

21. McDannell and Lang, *Heaven—A History*, 346.

22. Küng, *Eternal Life?*, quoting Bertolt Brecht, "Gegen Verführung," 22–23.

The Favorable Finale

A future as "brother . . . to the sluggish clod," in which there is "nothing," is *nothing* but the fatalistic imagination of minds that, though intelligent and well-meaning, refuse to accept the presence of a Sovereign God and his revelation of truth.

But that is not the finale offered by the Sovereign God. There is indeed a future life after bodily death. Human beings are immortal. Reflection and conversation about animal immortality is also pertinent. If it were not, there would be many fewer books on the shelves of philosophers, theologians, environmentalists, Christians, and serious seekers. Paper and ink have not been entirely wasted.

The conclusion of this particular inquiry must be built on definitions and explanations that are the most faithful to Scripture which in its fullness addresses the origin, purposes, and destiny of the cosmos, including human and animal. It affirms the value of both matter and spirit, in this present order of life and in the future restored world. With joy, the Scripture-based Christian can say,

> *When the perishable has been clothed with the imperishable, and the mortal with immortality, then the saying that is written will come true: Death has been swallowed up in victory!*[23]

The victory that Christ gives to believers is eternal life, which can be understood in three stages: 1) regeneration and forgiveness of sin in this earthly life, 2) freedom from sin and an individualized, conscious awareness and personal interaction with Christ and with other souls in an intermediate state between the death of the body and the final resurrection when Christ returns, and 3) the restoration of soul and body at that resurrection, followed by life in the *glorious freedom* of heavenly fellowship forever.

23. 1 Corinthians 15:54.

Animal Afterlife?

And the animals? *Their hope is assured.* Read Romans 8:21 again:

> *The creation itself will be delivered from its bondage to decay and brought into the glorious freedom of the children of God.*

Selected Bibliography

Abbott, Lyman. *The Theology of an Evolutionist.* Boston: Houghton Mifflin, 1897.

Adams, Charles Josiah. *Where Is My Dog? Or Is Man Alone Immortal?* New York: Fowler & Wells, 1892.

Ahlstrom, Sydney E. *A Religious History of the American People.* New Haven, CT: Yale University Press, 1972.

Alger, William R. *The Destiny of the Soul: A Critical History of the Doctrine of a Future Life.* 10th ed., with six new chapters, and a complete bibliography of the subject. Comprising 4,977 books relating to the nature, origin, and destiny of the soul, by Ezra Abbot. 1868. Reprint, New York: Greenwood, 1968.

Almond, Philip C. *Heaven and Hell in Enlightenment England.* Cambridge: Cambridge University Press, 1994.

Aquinas, Thomas. *Summa Theologiae: A Concise Translation.* Edited by Timothy McDermott. London: Eyre and Spottiswoode, 1989.

Armitage, Robert. *The Penscellwood Papers: Comprising Essays on the Souls and Future Life of Animals; on Capital Punishments; on the Evangelical Alliance; on the Endowment of the Protestant and Roman Catholic Churches of Ireland; and on the Education of the People.* London: Richard Bentley, 1846.

Armstrong, E. A. *St. Francis: Nature Mystic.* Berkeley, CA: University of California Press, 1973.

Augustine. *City of God.* Translated by Marcus Dods. Edinburgh: T. & T. Clark, 1913.

Axon, William E. A. *Shelley's Vegetarianism.* 1891. Reprint, New York: Haskell House, 1971.

Bayle, Pierre. *Historical and Critical Dictionary—Selections.* Translated by Richard Popkin. Indianapolis: Hackett, 1991.

Bede. *A History of the English Church and People.* Translated and with an introduction by Leo Sherley-Price. Baltimore: Penguin, 1955.

Bevan, J. O. *The Genesis and Evolution of the Individual Soul, Scientifically Treated, Including Also Problems Relating to Science and Immortality.* London: Williams & Norgate, 1909.

Boas, George. *The Happy Beast in French Thought of the 17th Century.* New York: Octagon, 1966.

Boettner, Loraine. *Immortality.* Philadelphia: Presbyterian and Reformed, 1956.

Bonnet, Charles. *La Palingénésie philosophique.* Paris, 1769.

Boucher de Perthes, Jacques. *De la Création. Essai sur l'Origine et la Progression des Etres.* Paris: Treuttel et Wurtz, Libraires, 1841.

Bozeman, Theodore Dwight. *Protestants in an Age of Science: The Baconian Ideal and Antebellum American Religious Thought.* Chapel Hill, NC: University of North Carolina Press, 1977.

Bradford, John. *Writings of John Bradford, Containing Sermons, Meditations, Examinations, etc.* 1555. Cambridge University Press, 1847. Reprint, New York: Johnson Reprint Corporation, 1968.

Bromiley, Geoffrey W., ed. *International Standard Bible Encyclopedia.* Grand Rapids: Eerdmans, 1995.

Brooks, Tracy Ane. *A Walk in Connection.* Bloomington, IN: Balboa, 2014.

Brown, Ira V. *Lyman Abbott, Christian Evolutionist.* Cambridge: Harvard University Press, 1953.

Brown, Jerry Wayne. *The Rise of Biblical Criticism in America, 1800–1870: The New England Scholars.* Middletown, CT: Wesleyan University Press, 1969.

Bryant, William Cullen. "Thanatopsis." In *Best Loved Poems*, edited by Richard C. MacKenzie, 109–11. New York: Permabooks, 1946.

Bucer, Martin. *Common Places of Martin Bucer.* Edited by David F. Wright. Abingdon, UK: Sutton Courtenay, 1972.

Buckner, Elijah D. *The Immortality of Animals and the Relation of Man as Guardian, from a Biblical and Philosophical Hypothesis.* Philadelphia: George W. Jacobs, 1903.

Buddemeyer-Porter, Mary. *Animals, Immortal Beings.* Wichita Falls, TX: Eden, 2005.

Bullock, C. Hassell. *An Introduction to the Old Testament Poetic Books.* Chicago: Moody, 1988.

Burns, James Drummond. *The Celestial City: Glimpses within the Gates.* Boston: American Tract Society, 1876.

Burtt, E. A. "The Metaphysical Newton." Originally in *The Metaphysical Foundations of Modern Physical Science* (1925), reprinted in *Science and Religious Belief: A Selection of Recent Historical Studies*, edited by C. A. Russell, 131–46. London: University of London Press, 1973.

Buswell, James Oliver. *A Systematic Theology of the Christian Religion.* Grand Rapids: Zondervan, 1962.

Butler, Joseph. *The Analogy of Religion Natural and Revealed.* London: J. M. Dent, 1906.

Calvin, John. *Institutes of the Christian Religion.* London: John Allen, 1813.

———. *Tracts and Treatises on the Reformation of the Church.* With a short life of Calvin by Theodore Beza. Translated from the original Latin by Henry Beveridge. Historical notes and introduction added to the present edition by Thomas F. Torrance. Grand Rapids: Eerdmans, 1958.

Campolo, Tony. *How To Rescue the Earth without Worshiping Nature.* Nashville: Thomas Nelson, 1992.

Candland, Douglas Keith. *Feral Children and Clever Animals.* Oxford: Oxford University Press, 1993.

Carson, Gerald. *Men, Beasts, and Gods: A History of Cruelty and Kindness to Animals.* New York: Scribner's Sons, 1972.

Carson, Rachel. *Silent Spring.* Boston: Houghton Mifflin, 1962.

Cesaresco, Evelyn Martinengo. "The Hebrew Concept of the Soul." *Open Court* XV (January 1901) 110–14.

Chadbourne, P. A. *Lectures on Natural Theology; or, Nature and the Bible.* New York: Putnam's Sons, 1867.

Chalmers, Thomas. *On the Power, Wisdom, and Goodness of God as Manifested in the Adaptation of External Nature to the Moral and Intellectual Constitution of Man.* London: William Pickering, 1833.

Charles, R. H. *Eschatology: The Doctrine of a Future Life in Israel, Judaism and Christianity.* New York: Schocken, 1963.

Chesterton, G. K. *Orthodoxy.* New York: John Lane, 1908.

Child, Addison. "Vitiated Moral Teaching." *Popular Science Monthly* 37.22 (July 1890) 408.

Clark, Gordon H. *The Biblical Doctrine of Man.* Jefferson, MD: Trinity Foundation, 1984.

———. *Lord God of Truth.* Hobbs, NM: Trinity Foundation, 1994.

———. *Thales to Dewey.* Boston: Houghton Mifflin, 1957.

Clark, Stephen R. L. *The Moral Status of Animals.* Oxford: Clarendon, 1977.

Clarke, Adam. *Commentary on the Bible.* Abridged by Ralph Earle. Grand Rapids: Baker, 1967.

Clarke, R. F. "On Cruelty to Animals in Its Moral Aspect." *The Month and Catholic Review* VI (Sept-Dec 1875) 393–406.

Cobbe, Frances Power. *An Essay on Intuitive Morals.* London: Trubner, 1864.

———. *Concerning Immortality.* Chicago: n.p., 1888.

Cochrane, Arthur C., ed. *Reformed Confessions of the Sixteenth Century.* With Historical Introductions by A. C. Cochrane. Philadelphia: Westminster, 1966.

Conser, Walter H. *God and the Natural World: Religion and Science in Antebellum America.* Columbia: University of South Carolina Press, 1993.

Confession of Faith, The: Agreed upon by the Assembly of Divines at Westminster. The Larger Catechism. The Shorter Catechism. The Directory for Publick Worship. The Form of Presbyterial Church Government. With References to the Proofs from the Scripture. Edinburgh: Blackwood & Sons, 1957.

Copleston, Frederick. *History of Philosophy.* New York: Image, 1962.

Cournot, A. A. *Matérialisme, Vitalisme, Rationalisme.* Paris: Hachette, 1923.

Cowper, William. *Poetical Works of William Cowper.* With Notes and a Memoir by John Bruce. London: Bell and Daldy, 1866.

Cullman, Oscar. *Immortality of the Soul or Resurrection of the Dead? The Witness of the New Testament.* New York: Macmillan, 1958.

Cummings, G. Duncan. *When You Go to Heaven.* Los Altos, CA: Published by the author, 1921.

Cunningham, Laurence. *St. Francis of Assisi.* Boston: Twayne, 1976.

Darwin, Charles. *The Expressions of the Emotions in Man and Animals.* New York: Appleton, 1898.

———. *The Origin of Species and The Descent of Man.* New York: The Modern Library, Random House, 1936.

Dawson, Virginia P. "The Problem of Soul in the 'little machines' of Réaumur and Charles Bonnet." *Eighteenth-Century Studies* 18.4 (1985) 503–22.

Dean, Richard. *An Essay on the Future Life of Brutes, Introduced with Observations upon EVIL, Its Nature, and Origin.* Vol. 2. Manchester: J. Harrop, 1767.

de Chardin, Pierre Teilhard. *Hymn of the Universe.* New York: Harper & Row, 1961.

Delumeau, Jean. *Une Histoire du Paradis: Le Jardin des Délices.* Paris: Fayard, 1992.

DeWitt, Calvin B., ed. *The Environment and the Christian: What Does the New Testament Say about the Environment?* Grand Rapids: Baker, 1991.

Dillenberger, Jane, and Joshua Taylor. *The Hand and the Spirit: Religious Art in America, 1700–1900.* Berkeley, CA: University Art Museum, 1972.

Dillenberger, John. *Protestant Thought and Natural Science: A Historical Interpretation.* 1960. Reprint, Westport, CT: Greenwood, 1977.

Donnelly, John Patrick. *Robert Bellarmine, Spiritual Writings.* New York: Paulist, 1989.

Douglas, J. D., Earle E. Cairns, and James E. Ruark, eds. *The New International Dictionary of the Christian Church.* Grand Rapids: Zondervan, 1974.

Drummond, William H. *The Rights of Animals, and Man's Obligation to Treat Them with Humanity.* London: John Mardon, 1838.

Dubos, René. *So Human an Animal.* New York: Scribner's Sons, 1968.

Dupree, Hunter. *Asa Gray, 1810–888.* Cambridge, MA: Belknap, 1959.

Edwards, Jonathan. *The Works of Jonathan Edwards.* Edinburgh: Banner of Truth Trust, 1984.

Emerson, R. W. *The Complete Essays and Other Writings of Ralph Waldo Emerson.* Edited by Brooks Atkinson. New York: The Modern Library, 1940.

———. *Nature.* With introduction by Warner Berthoff. San Francisco: Chandler, 1968.

Evans, E. P. *The Criminal Prosecution and Capital Punishment of Animals.* London: Faber & Faber, 1906.

———. *Evolutional Ethics and Animal Psychology.* New York: D. Appleton, 1898.

Fairholme, Edward G., and Wellesley Pain. *A Century of Work for Animals: The History of the R.S.P.C.A., 1824–1924.* New York: Dutton, 1924.

Fallows, Samuel, Dwight L. Moody, Charles H. Spurgeon, T. D. Talmage, and four hundred other prominent thinkers and writers. With an introduction by the Rt. Rev. Samuel Fallows. *The Home Beyond, or, Views of Heaven and Its Relation to Earth.* Chicago: Coburn and Newman, 1884.

Fallows, Samuel, Andrew Zenos, and Herbert Willett, eds. *The Popular and Critical Bible Encyclopaedia and Scriptural Dictionary.* Chicago: Howard-Severance, 1901.

Farrar, Canon Richard. *What Heaven Is.* New York: H. M. Caldwell, 1897.

Feuerbach, Ludwig. *The Essence of Christianity.* Translated from the German by George Eliot, with an introductory essay by Karl Barth and foreword by H. Richard Niebuhr. New York: Harper & Row, 1957.

Figuier, Louis. *The Tomorrow of Death; or, The Future Life According to Science.* Boston: Roberts Brothers, 1872.

Fiske, John. *Outlines of Cosmic Philosophy, Based on the Doctrine of Evolution, with Criticisms on the Positive Philosophy.* Boston: Houghton Mifflin, 1874.

———. *Through Nature to God.* Boston: Houghton Mifflin, 1899.

———. *The Unseen World.* Boston: Houghton Mifflin, 1876.

Finkelstein, J. J. "The Ox That Gored." *Transactions of the American Philosophical Society* 71.2 (1981) 1–89.

Flourens, Pierre Marie Jean. *De l'Instinct et de l'intelligence des animaux.* 4th ed. Paris: Louis Hachette, 1861.

Forde, Gerhard O. "Romans 8:18–27." *Interpretation* 38.3 (1984) 281–89.

Fowle, T. W. *The Reconciliation of Religion and Science, Being Essays on Immortality, Inspiration, Miracles, and the Being of Christ.* London: H. S. King, 1873.

———. "Science and Immortality." *Popular Science Monthly* 27 (May 1872) 26–40.

Francis of Assisi. *The Little Flowers of St. Francis.* Translated by Roger Hudleston, with an Introduction by Paulinus Lavery. Westminster, MD: Newman, 1953.

———. *The Writings of St. Francis of Assisi.* Translated by Benen Fahy, with an introduction and notes by Placid Hermann. Chicago: Herald, 1963.

French, Richard D. *Antivivisection and Medical Science in Victorian Society.* Princeton: Princeton University Press, 1975.

Frey, R. G. *Interests and Rights: The Case against Animals.* Oxford: Clarendon, 1980.

The Fundamentals: A Testimony to the Truth. Edited by R. A. Torrey, A. C. Dixon, et al. 1917. Reprint, Grand Rapids: Baker, 1988.

Gentry, Thomas G. *Life and Immortality, or Soul in Plants and Animals.* Philadelphia: Burk & McFetridge, 1897 (Republished as *Intelligence in Plants and Animals.* New York: Doubleday, 1900.)

Gerstner, John H. *Jonathan Edwards on Heaven and Hell.* Grand Rapids: Baker, 1980.

Girard, Marc. *Louange Cosmique: Bible et animisme*. Tournai et Montreal: Desclie et Bellarmin, 1973.

Godet, F. *Commentary on St. Paul's Epistle to the Romans*. Edinburgh: T. & T. Clark, 1892.

Goodall, Jane. *Hope for Animals and Their World*. New York: Grand Central, 2009.

Goodman, Godfrey. *The Creatures Praysing God*. London: 1622. Reprint, Norwood, NJ: Johnson, 1979.

Gray, Asa. *Darwiniana: Essays and Reviews Pertaining to Darwinism*. 1876. Reprint, Cambridge, MA: Belknap, 1963.

Greene, John C. *Death of Adam: Evolution and Its Impact on Western Thought*. Ames, IA: Iowa State University Press, 1959.

———. *Science, Ideology, and World View: Essays in the History of Evolutionary Ideas*. Berkeley, CA: University of California Press, 1981.

Haller, John S., Jr. *Fictions of Certitude: Science, Faith, and the Search for Meaning, 1840–920*. Tuscaloosa, AL: University of Alabama Press, 2020.

———. "The Great Biologic Problem: Vitalism, Materialism, and the Philosophy of Organism." *New York State Journal of Medicine* 86.2 (1986) 81–88.

———. *Swedenborg's Principles of Usefulness: Social Reform Thought from the Enlightenment to American Pragmatism*. West Chester, PA: Swedenborg Foundation, 2020.

Harbaugh, Henry. *The Heavenly Home, or, The Employments and Enjoyments of the Saints in Heaven*. Philadelphia: Lindsay & Blakiston, 1853.

Hartley, Lodwick Charles. *William Cowper, Humanitarian*. Chapel Hill, NC: University of North Carolina Press, 1938.

Hartshorne, Charles. "In Defense of Wordsworth's View of Nature." *Philosophy and Literature* 4.1 (1980) 80–85.

Hasker, William. "Souls of Beasts and Men." *Religious Studies* 10.3 (1974) 265–77.

Hastings, Hester. *Man and Beast in French Thought of the Eighteenth Century*. Baltimore: Johns Hopkins, 1936.

Hawkins, T. S. *The Soul of an Animal*. London: Allen & Unwin, 1921.

Hendrick, George. *Henry Salt: Humanitarian Reformer and Man of Letters*. Urbana, IL: University of Illinois Press, 1977.

Hendry, George S. *Theology of Nature*. Philadelphia: Westminster, 1980.

Henry, Matthew. *Commentary on the Whole Bible*. Marshallton, DE: National Foundation for Christian Education, photolithographed from Fisher Edition, London, 1845.

———. *Commentary on the Whole Bible*. Grand Rapids: Zondervan, 1960.

Himmelfarb, Gertrude. *Darwin and the Darwinian Revolution*. Garden City, NY: Doubleday, 1959.

Hobhouse, L. T. *Mind in Evolution*. London: Macmillan, 1901.

Hodge, Charles. *Commentary on the Epistle to the Romans*. 1835. Reprint, London: Banner of Truth Trust, 1983.

———. *Systematic Theology*. 1872–73. Reprint, Grand Rapids: Eerdmans, 1952.

———. *What Is Darwinism?* New York: Scribners, Armstrong, 1874.

Hovencamp, Herbert. *Science and Religion in America, 1800–1860*. Philadelphia: University of Pennsylvania Press, 1978.

Hughes, Philip E., ed. *Creative Minds in Contemporary Theology*. Grand Rapids: Eerdmans, 1966.

Hume, Charles W. *The Status of Animals in the Christian Religion*. London: Universities Federation for Animal Welfare, 1956.

Humphry, William Gilson. *The Doctrine of a Future State: In nine sermons preached before the University of Cambridge in the year M.DCCC.XLIX at the lecture founded by the Rev. John Hulse*. London: John W. Parker, 1850.

Huxley, Thomas H. *Man's Place in Nature*. Ann Arbor, MI: University of Michigan Press, 1959.

———. *Physiography: An Introduction to the Study of Nature*. New York: Appleton, 1878.

———. *Science and Christian Tradition: Essays*. New York: Appleton, 1894.

International Standard Bible Encyclopedia. Edited by Geoffrey W. Bromiley. Grand Rapids: Eerdmans, 1995.

Isidore of Seville. *Etymologiae*. First published in Spain between 600–625. Modern version edited by Wallace Lindsay. Oxford: Oxford University Press, 1911.

Kaplan, Helmut F. "Do Animals Have Souls?" *Between Species* 7.3 (1991) 138–47.

Kaiser, Christopher B. *Creation and the History of Science*. Grand Rapids: Eerdmans, 1991.

Kerr, Hugh Thomson, Jr. *A Compend of Luther's Theology*. Philadelphia: Westminster, 1943.

Kirby, William. *On the Power, Wisdom, and Goodness of God as Manifested in the Creation of Animals and in Their History, Habits, and Instincts*. London: William Pickering, 1835.

Kowalski, Gary A. *The Souls of Animals*. Walpole, NH: Stillpoint, 1991.

Küng, Hans. *Eternal Life? Life After Death as a Medical, Philosophical, and Theological Problem*. Translation by Edward Quinn. Garden City, NY: Doubleday, 1984.

LeConte, Joseph. *Evolution: Its Nature, Its Evidences, and Its Relation to Religious Thought*. New York: Appleton, 1888.

Lewis, C. S. *The Problem of Pain*. New York: Macmillan, 1962.

Lindberg, David C., and Ronald L. Numbers. *God and Nature: Historical Essays on the Encounter between Christianity and Science*. Berkeley: University of California Press, 1986.

Linzey, Andrew. *Animal Theology*. London: SCM, 1994.

Linzey, Andrew, and Tom Regan, eds. *Animals and Christianity: A Book of Readings*. New York: Crossroad, 1988.

Little Flowers of St. Francis of Assisi. Translated by Roger Hudleston, with an introduction by Paulinus Lavery. Westminster, MD: Newman, 1953.

Lovejoy, Arthur O. *The Great Chain of Being: A Study of the History of an Idea.* Cambridge: Harvard University Press, 1966.

Lovejoy, Arthur O., and George Boas. *Primitivism and Related Ideas in Antiquity.* New York: Octagon, 1965.

Luther, Martin. *Lectures on Romans.* Translated and edited by Wilhelm Pauck. Library of Christian Classics, Vol. 15. Philadelphia: Westminster, 1961.

———. *Luther's Works.* Volume I, *Lectures on Genesis, Chapters 1–5.* Edited by Jaroslav Pelikan. St. Louis: Concordia, 1958.

———. *The Table Talk of Martin Luther.* Translated and edited by William Hazlitt. London: George Bell and Sons, 1902.

Mangin, Arthur. *L'Homme et la Bête, ouvrage illustré de cent vingt gravures.* Paris: Librairie de Firmin Didot Frères, Fils, et Cie., 1872.

Manning, Aubrey, and James Serpell, eds. *Animals and Human Society: Changing Perspectives.* London: Routledge, 1994.

Marais, Eugene. *The Soul of the Ape.* Introduction by Robert Ardrey. New York: Atheneum, 1969.

MacDonald, Gregory (pseudonym for Robin Parry). *The Evangelical Universalist.* Eugene, OR: Wipf and Stock, 2006.

McCosh, James. *Our Moral Nature, Being a Brief System of Ethics.* New York: Scribner's Sons, 1892.

McCrea, Roswell C. *The Humane Movement: A Descriptive Survey.* New York: The Columbia University Press, 1910.

McDannell, Colleen, and Bernhard Lang. *Heaven—A History.* New Haven, CT: Yale University Press, 1988.

McLaren, Alexander, and Canon Liddon, D. L. Moody, C. H. Spurgeon, T. D. Talmage. *A Symposium: The Resurrection.* New York: Fleming H. Revell, 1896.

Menault, Ernest. *L'Intelligence des Animaux.* Paris: Librairie de L. Hachette et Cie., 1869.

Midgley, Mary. *Animals and Why They Matter.* Athens: University of Georgia Press, 1983.

———. *Beast and Man: The Roots of Human Nature.* Hassocks, UK: Harvester, 1979.

Montaigne, Michel de. *Essays.* Translated with an introduction by J. M. Cohen. London: Penguin, 1958.

Montgomery, Sy. *Soul of an Octopus.* New York: Simon & Schuster, 2015.

Moore, James R. *The Post-Darwinian Controversies: A Study of the Protestant Struggle to Come to Terms with Darwin in Great Britain and America, 1870–1900.* Cambridge: Cambridge University Press, 1979.

Morgan, Conwy Lloyd. *The Animal Mind.* London: Edward Arnold, 1930.

Morris, Francis Orpen. *Records of Animal Sagacity and Character.* With a Preface on the Future Existence of the Animal Creation. London: Longman, Green, Longman, and Roberts, 1861.

Morris, M. C. F. *Francis Orpen Morris: A Memoir.* London: John C. Nimmo, 1897.

Mourant, John A. *Augustine on Immortality*. Villanova, PA: Villanova University Press, 1969.

Muckermann, Hermann, S.J. *The Humanizing of the Brute, or The Essential Difference between the Human and Animal Soul Proved from their Specific Activities*. St. Louis: Herder, 1906.

Munday, John C., Jr. "Creature Mortality: From Creation or the Fall?" *Journal of the Evangelical Theological Society* 35.1 (1992) 51–68.

Murray, John. *The Epistle to the Romans*. Grand Rapids: Eerdmans, 1959.

Myers, Frederic W. H. *Science and a Future Life, with other Essays*. London: Macmillan, 1893.

Nash, James A. *Loving Nature: Ecological Integrity and Christian Responsibility*. Nashville: Abingdon, 1991.

Nash, Roderick F. *The Rights of Nature: A History of Environmental Ethics*. Madison, WI: University of Wisconsin Press, 1989.

Netter, Abraham. *L'Homme et l'animal devant la méthode expérimentale*. Paris: E. Dentu, 1882.

Niven, Charles D. *History of the Humane Movement*. London: Johnson, 1967.

Noll, Mark A., ed. *The Princeton Theology, 1812–1921: Scripture, Science, and Theological Method from Archibald Alexander to Benjamin B. Warfield*. Grand Rapids: Baker, 1983.

Numbers, Ronald L. "George Frederick Wright: From Christian Darwinist to Fundamentalist." *Isis* 79.4 (1988) 624–45.

Osler, William. *Science and Immortality*. Boston: Houghton Mifflin, 1905.

Pelikan, Jaroslav. *The Christian Tradition: A History of the Development of Doctrine and Emergence of the Catholic Tradition*. Chicago: The University of Chicago Press, 1971.

Penelhum, Terence. *Butler*. London: Routledge & Kegan Paul, 1985.

———. *Immortality*. Belmont, CA: Wordsworth, 1973.

Peters, Madison Clinton. *Hebrew Hopes of Heaven: What the Old Testament Has to Say about the Great Hereafter*. San Francisco: Jewish Times, 1911.

Pilcher, Charles V. *The Hereafter in Jewish and Christian Thought*. New York: Macmillan, 1940.

Pinney, Roy. *The Animals in the Bible: The Identity and Natural History of All the Animals Mentioned in the Bible*. Philadelphia: Chilton, 1964.

Preece, Rod, and Lorna Chamberlain. *Animal Welfare and Human Values*. Waterloo, ON: Wilfrid Laurier University Press, 1993.

Prewitt, Page. "One Woman's Answer." *The Intercessor* 37.1 (2021) 8–11.

Prichard, J. C. *A Review of the Doctrine of a Vital Principle as Maintained by Some Writers on Physiology with Observations on the Causes of Physical and Animal Life*. London: Sherwood, Gilbert, and Piper, 1829.

Psychology: or A Review of the Arguments Deducible from Philosophy and Tradition. In Proof of the Existence and Immortality of the Animal Soul. London: J. B. Nichols & Son, 1831.

Quinn, Edward. "Animals in Heaven." *New Blackfriars* 65.767 (1984) 224–26.

Radner, Daisie, and Michael Radner. *Animal Consciousness*. Buffalo, NY: Prometheus, 1989.

Regan, Tom. *The Case for Animals Rights.* London: Kegan Paul, 1984.

Ritvo, Harriet. *The Animal Estate: The English and Other Creatures in the Victorian Age.* Cambridge: Harvard University Press, 1987.

Romanes, George John. *Animal Intelligence.* New York: D. Appleton, 1883.

Root, Andrew. *The Grace of Dogs.* New York: Convergent, 2017.

Rosenfield, L. D. C. *From Beast-Machine to Man-Machine: Animal Soul in French Letters from Descartes to LaMettrie.* 1940. Reprint, Hemel Hempstead, UK: Octagon, 1968.

Roszak, Theodore. *Unfinished Animal: The Aquarian Frontier and the Evolution of Consciousness.* New York: Harper & Row, 1975.

Rothschild, Miriam. *Animals and Man.* Oxford: Clarendon, 1986.

Royce, Josiah. *The Conception of Immortality.* Westport, CT: Greenwood, 1900.

Rudwick, Martin J. S. "Shape and Meaning of Earth History." *God and Nature: Historical Essays and the Encounter between Christianity and Science,* edited by David C. Lindberg and Ronald Numbers. Berkeley, CA: University of California Press, 1986.

Runes, Dagobert. *Dictionary of Philosophy.* New York: Philosophical Library, 1960.

Russell, Colin A., ed. *The Earth, Humanity, and God.* London: UCL, 1994.

———. *Science and Religious Belief: A Selection of Recent Historical Studies.* London: University of London Press, 1973.

Salmond, Stewart D. F. *The Christian Doctrine of Immortality.* Edinburgh: T. & T. Clark, 1897.

Salt, Henry S. *Animals' Rights Considered in Relation to Social Progress.* London: Macmillan, 1894.

Sandeen, Ernest R. *The Roots of Fundamentalism: British and American Millenarianism, 1800–1830.* Chicago: University of Chicago Press, 1970.

Sapontzis, S. F. *Morals, Reason, and Animals.* Philadelphia: Temple University Press, 1987.

Schaeffer, Francis A. *Pollution and the Death of Man: The Christian View of Ecology.* Wheaton, IL: Tyndale, 1970.

Schaff, Philip. *History of the Christian Church.* Grand Rapids: Eerdmans, 1960.

Schochet, Elijah Judah. *Animal Life in Jewish Tradition: Attitudes and Relationships.* New York: KTAV, 1984.

Schweitzer, Albert. *The Animal World of Albert Schweitzer: Jungle Insights into Reverence for Life.* Translated and edited by Charles R. Joy. Boston: Beacon, 1951.

Shelley, Percy Bysshe. *Two Essays on Vegetarianism: A Vindication of Natural Diet and On the Vegetable System of Diet.* 1884. Reprint, Folcroft, PA: Folcroft Library, 1975.

———. *A Vindication of Natural Diet.* London: Smith and Davy, 1813.

Singer, Peter. *Animal Liberation.* New York: Avon, 1975.

Smart, Christopher. *Jubilate Agno. Rejoice in the Lamb: A Song from Bedlam.* Edited by W. F. Stead. London: Jonathan Cape, 1939.

————. *The Poetical Works of Christopher Smart*. Edited by Karina Williamson. Oxford: Clarendon, 1980.

Smith, Emily Mary. *The Investigation of Mind in Animals*. Cambridge: University Press, 1915.

Smith, Wilbur. *The Biblical Doctrine of Heaven*. Chicago: Moody, 1968.

Smyth, Newman. *The Religious Feeling: A Study for Faith*. New York: Scribner, Armstrong, 1878.

Sobol, Peter Gordon. *John Buridan on the Soul and Sensation: An Edition of Book II of His Commentary on Aristotle's Book of the Soul*. Bloomington, IN: Indiana University Press, 1984.

Sorabji, Richard. *Animal Minds and Human Morals: The Origins of the Western Debate*. Ithaca, NY: Cornell University Press, 1993.

Southgate, Christopher. *The Groaning of Creation: God, Evolution, and the Problem of Evil*. Louisville, KY: Westminster John Knox, 2008.

Spencer, Hazelton, ed. *British Literature, Vol. II: From Blake to the Present Day*. Boston: Heath, 1952.

Sproul, R. C. *Now That's a Good Question*. Wheaton, IL: Tyndale House, 1996.

Spurgeon, Charles H. *Metropolitan Tabernacle Pulpit*. Pasadena, TX: Pilgrim, 1969.

Steel, Flora A. W. *A Book of Mortals: Being a record of the good deeds and good qualities of what humanity is pleased to call the lower animals*. London: William Heinemann, 1905.

Steinsaltz, Adin. *The Essential Talmud*. New York: Basic, 1976.

Stephens, Lester D. *Joseph LeConte, Gentle Prophet of Evolution*. Baton Rouge, LA: Louisiana State University Press, 1982.

Strauss, David F. *The Life of Jesus Critically Examined*. London: Swan Sonnenschein, 1902.

Street, J. R. "A Genetic Study of Immortality." PhD diss, Clark University, Worcester, MA, 1893.

Street, Jacob Richard. "A Genetic Study of Immortality." *Pedagogical Seminary & Journal of Genetic Psychology* 6 (1899) 267–313.

Streeter, B. H., A. Clutton-Brock, C. W. Emmet, and J. A. Hadfield. *Immortality: An Essay in Discovery Co-ordinating Scientific, Psychical, and Biblical Research*. 1917. Reprint, London: Macmillan, 1930.

Stromberg, Roland N. *European Intellectual History Since 1789*. Englewood Cliffs, NJ: Prentice Hall, 1994.

Swedenborg, Emanuel. *Arcana Coelestia: The Heavenly Arcana*. New York: The American Swedenborg Printing and Publishing Society, 1915.

————. *Heaven and Its Wonders and Hell, from Things Heard and Seen*. 1758. Reprint, New York: Swedenborg Foundation, 1952.

Thomas, Keith. *Wordsworth and Philosophy: Empiricism and Transcendentalism in the Poetry*. Ann Arbor, MI: UMI Research Press, 1989.

Thompson, Augustus Charles. *The Better Land; or, The Believer's Journey and Future Home*. Boston: Gould and Lincoln, 1854.

Thorndike, Edward L. *Animal Intelligence: Experimental Studies*. New York: Macmillan, 1911.

Toogood, John. *A Discourse on Some of Those Instances of the Power, Wisdom, and Goodness of God, Which Are Within the Reach of Common Observation, to which is added, The Duty of Mercy, and Sin of Cruelty to Brutes; taken chiefly from Dr. Primatt's dissertation.* 4th ed. Boston: Samuel Hall, 1802.

Turner, James. *Reckoning with the Beast: Animals, Pain, and Humanity in the Victorian Mind.* Baltimore: The Johns Hopkins University Press, 1980.

Torrey, Reuben A., ed. *The Fundamentals.* Grand Rapids: Baker, 1988.

Tylor, Edward B. *Primitive Culture.* London: John Murray, 1891.

Vartier, Jean. *Les Procès d'animaux du moyen âge à nos jours.* Paris: Louis Hachette, 1970.

Verlaine, Louis. *L'Âme des bêtes: quelques pages d'histoire.* Paris: F. Alcan, 1931.

Warren, George. *A Disquisition on the Nature and Properties of Living Animals with An Inquiry How Far Our Knowledge of Anatomy and Physiology Is Consistent with the Belief of a Soul and a Future Life, and on the Intellectual Difference between Man and Brutes.* London: Longman, Rees, Orme, Brown, and Green, 1828.

Watson, John S. *The Reasoning Power in Animals.* London: Reeve, 1867.

Webb, Stephen. *On God and Dogs: A Christian Theology of Compassion for Animals.* Oxford: Oxford University Press, 1998.

Wertheim, Jon. "The 1925 Nome Serum Run." *The Daily Cover,* January 13, 2021.

Werther, David. "Animal Reason and the Imago Dei." *Religious Studies* 24.3 (1988) 325–35.

Wesley, John. *Explanatory Notes upon the New Testament.* New York: Nelson & Phillips, 1754.

———. *The Works of John Wesley: Sermons on Several Occasions.* Grand Rapids: Zondervan, 1872.

Wildiers, N. Max. *The Theologian and His Universe: Theology and Cosmology from the Middle Ages to the Present.* New York: Seabury, 1982.

Willey, Basil. *Darwin and Butler: Two Versions of Evolution.* New York: Harcourt, Brace, 1960.

———. *Nineteenth Century Studies: Coleridge to Matthew Arnold.* New York: Columbia University Press, 1949.

Wilson, Geoffrey B. *Romans: A Digest of Reformed Comment.* Edinburgh: Banner of Truth Trust, 1977.

Winsten, Stephen. *Salt and His Circle.* New York: Hutchinson, 1951.

Wolf, William J. *Thoreau: Mystic, Prophet, Ecologist.* Philadelphia: United Church, 1974.

Wood, John George. *Man and Beast, Here and Hereafter.* New York: Harper, 1875.

Wordsworth, William. *Selected Poems and Prefaces.* Edited by Jack Stillinger. Boston: Houghton Mifflin, 1965.

Youatt, William. *The Obligation and Extent of Humanity to Brutes, Principally Considered with Reference to the Domesticated Animals.* London: Longman, Orme, Brown, Green and Longman, 1839.

Youmans, Edward L. "Editor's Table." *Popular Science Monthly* I and III (1872).

Author and Subject Index

intelligence, 4, 9, 10–12, 30, 31, 35, 36, 57, 62, 64, 66, 70, 112, 121, 124, 126, 127
International Standard Bible Encyclopedia, 103, 104, 118, 123
Isidore, 39, 123

James, William, 88
Jerome, 35
Jesus Christ, 23, 24, 33–34, 43, 44, 57, 59, 63, 69, 71, 76, 90, 91, 95, 99, 100, 101, 107, 108, 109, 115, 121
John, 24
Jonah, 19, 105
Jonas, Hans, 114
Joshua, 18
Jubilate Agno, 63–64, 126
Justin Martyr, 35

Kant, Immanuel, 85
Keats, John, 86
Kepler, Johannes, 74
Keswick Convention, 96
Kirby, William, 76, 123
Kowalski, Gary, 8, 111–12, 123

Lamartine, Alphonse de, 86
Lang, Bernhard, 101, 114, 124
LeConte, Joseph, 91–92, 97, 123
Lewis, C.S., 111, 123
Luke, 4
Luther, Martin, 51–52, 113, 123, 124

MacDonald, Gregory, 35, 124
MacDougall, Duncan, 80–81
Malebranche, Nicolas, 66, 73
Manasseh, Rabbi, 66
Mani, Manichaeans, 34
Mangin, Arthur, 8, 40, 124
Marais, E., 8, 124
Marcion, 34
Marcus Aurelius, 32
Martin, Richard, 89–90

Mary I, Queen of England, 53
materialism, 32, 81, 113, 114, 119, 122
McDannell, Colleen, 101, 114, 124
metempsychosis, 29
Michelet, Jules, 86, 95
millennium, 19, 32, 38, 100–101, 103
Miller, Perry, 67
Mission: Wolf, 3, 4
Montgomery, Sy, 8, 112, 124
Moody, Dwight L., 102, 118, 121, 124, 127
moral behavior, 40
moral sense, 8, 9, 11–12
Moses, 8, 16, 104
Myers, F.W.H., 81, 125

Nash, Roderick, 67, 125
nephesh, 24–26
New Age, 103
Newton, Isaac, 74, 75, 118
Nome Serum Run, 110, 128

Offray, Julien, 73
Origen, 34–35, 65
Oswald, King of Northumbria, 39–40

Paley, William, 75
Parker, Theodore, 97
Parry, Robin, xii, 124
Patrick, St., 36–37, 39
Paul, St., x, 22, 23, 33–34, 53, 56, 68, 69, 122
Penda, King of Mercia, 39
Penulhum, Terence, 61
Peter, 58
Philo, 34, 65
Pilcher, C.V., 21, 125
Plato, 8, 29–30, 31, 34, 103
Plotinus, 32
Prewitt, Page, 8, 125
Prichard, J.C., 11, 125
Primatt, Humphry, 89, 128
Princeton Presbyterians, 77, 96, 98, 125

Scripture Index

www.ingramcontent.com/pod-product-compliance
Lightning Source LLC
Chambersburg PA
CBHW070739030726
47601CB00001B/78